BRITISH RAILWAYS

PAST and PRESENT

No 10

GW00514795

FRONT COVER:

NORTHAMPTON CASTLE: Crosti-boilered 2-10-0 No 92024 heads south on a coal train on 17 June 1961. All the Crosti-boilered examples of this class were Wellingborough-based engines for many years and this one was sent new from Crewe Works to 15A in June 1955. It ended its days at Birkenhead, withdrawal taking place in November 1967. *Michael Mensing*

On 8 June 1988 electric multiple unit No 310076 leaves Northampton on the 16.06 to Euston. Compare the two photographs and spot the similarities — gone, however, are the water tower and old station buildings. This class of multiple unit has now been phased out of working Northampton/Euston locals, being replaced by the new-style Class '321' EMU. This particular example still works on the LMR around the Birmingham area and has been refurbished and renumbered No 310103.

REAR COVER:

WIGSTON SOUTH JUNCTION on Saturday 22 August 1959. The line coming in from the left is the south curve joining the Birmingham line to the Midland (see page 26), opened in 1872. Also to the left are the carriage sidings which provided stock for all the local workings from Leicester. Over to the right is a row of houses built for the local railwaymen by the Midland. Stanier '8F' 2-8-0 No 48657 plods south past the signal box with a coal train; this engine bowed out to modernisation in October 1964, its last depot being Bletchley. *Michael Mensing*

The same location on 21 October 1988. The railway cottages remain, but most other items of railway interest have gone. The south curve is now a single line and nearly all the sidings have been taken up. The impressive signal box, and with it the manual signalling, has disappeared. Class '37' No 37428 *David Lloyd George* heads the 15.30 Fridays-only Derby to St Pancras.

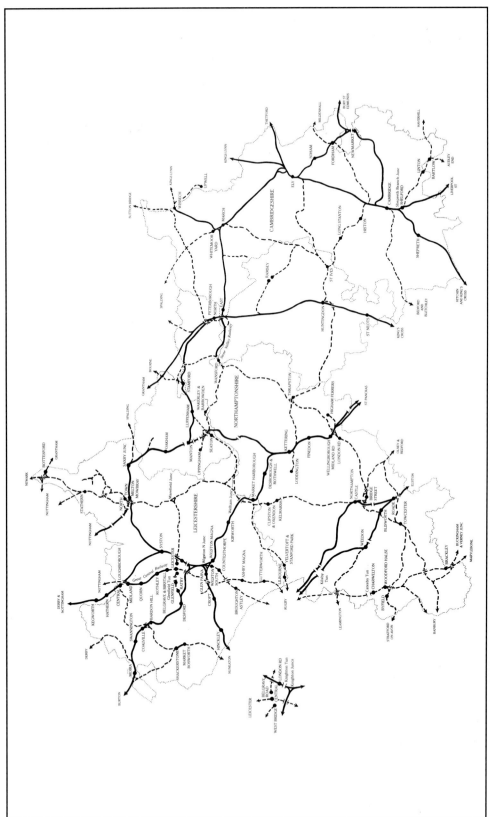

BRITISH RAILWAYS PAST & PRESENT No 10: THE EAST MIDLANDS — This book represents a detailed examination of the changing face of the region depicted in this sketch map. The pictures have been chosen to provide a balanced view, including railways which are still in use or being developed as the book goes to press, together with scenes of railways that have been closed and either abandoned or redeveloped since the 'past' pictures were taken.

PAST and PRESENT

No 10

The East Midlands

Leicestershire, Northamptonshire and Cambridgeshire

Chris Milner & Chris Banks

Past & Present Publishing Ltd

© Chris Milner and Chris Banks 1991

Note: All the 'present' photographs have been taken by Chris Milner unless otherwise credited; All other credits refer to the photographers of the 'past' views. All research and captions are by Chris Banks.

All rights reserved. No part of this publication may be reproduced, stored in a retrieval system or transmitted, in any form or by any means, electronic, mechanical, photocopying, recording or otherwise, without prior permission in writing from Past & Present Publishing Ltd.

First published in September 1991
Reprinted October 1993

British Library Cataloguing in Publication Data

Milner Chris, 1952–
British railways past and present.
    No. 10: The East Midlands.
    I. Title II. Banks, Chris
    385.0941

ISBN 1 85895 011 2

Past & Present Publishing Ltd
Unit 5
Home Farm Close
Church Street
Wadenhoe
Peterborough PE8 5TE
Tel/fax (08015) 4-4-0

Printed and bound in Great Britain

PETERBOROUGH NORTH (see also pages 104-6): The Great Northern opened its line to this station on 5 August 1850 from Maiden Lane, London, and the line opened north to Retford on 15 July 1852 for freight and 1 August for passengers. This view, recorded on Whit Monday, 6 June 1960, has Gresley 'A4' 4-6-2 No 60031 *Golden Plover* arriving on the 09.30 Glasgow Queen Street to King's Cross. The awkward layout with speed restricted curves was a handicap to fast timings for many years. No 60031 was a survivor until 1965, its last duties being as a frequent performer on the Glasgow Buchanan Street to Dundee turns. By October it was out of use at Glasgow St Rollox shed and was finally withdrawn on the 29th. *Michael Mensing*

The rebuilt Peterborough station is seen on 10 September 1988. The layout has been completely altered and electrified, and is now laid out for high-speed running on the through lines. HST power car No 43197 heads the 13.35 Newcastle to King's Cross.

CONTENTS

LEICESTER LONDON ROAD on Wednesday 8 August 1956. Standing in the No 2 down platform is LMS '2P' 4-4-0 No 40690 and BR Standard '5MT' 4-6-0 No 73016 on the northbound 'Thames-Clyde Express'. No 40690 dated back to 1932 and was part of a batch built at Crewe. It was withdrawn in December 1960 from Leeds Holbeck shed. No 73016 was built in September 1951 at Derby and was first allocated to Sheffield Grimesthorpe. Withdrawal came in December 1966 from Weymouth. *Ken Hunt*

On Thursday 10 May 1990 Class '47' No 47569 stands at platform 2 on a northbound parcels. The old station was swept away in a total rebuild completed in 1985. More recent alterations have been the removal of the centre road, replaced with flowerbeds, and the new footbridge linking the car park to the station platforms.

INTRODUCTION

The Midlands and East Anglia have always had strong links in railway matters, so for this volume in the 'Past and Present' series it is natural that the areas we are considering should be together. The counties of Leicestershire, Northamptonshire and Cambridgeshire are the subjects of our investigations, which have resulted in some surprising discoveries.

The three counties offer a wide variety of contrast, with the landscape changing from industrial to agricultural the further east one travels. During the 1950s and 1960s the annual exodus from Leicester to the East Coast resorts of Skegness and Yarmouth at holiday times forged a strong association with the railway across the area, with specials operating from Leicester Belgrave Road and later London Road. Saturday specials still run in the summer and for many years have allowed the unusual sight of pairs of Class '20' diesel locomotives providing the motive power. The daily service from Birmingham to Norwich, Cambridge and now Stansted Airport continues the association with this cross-country route. Class '31' diesel locomotives with five coaches were, for many years, the usual formation, interspersed with first-generation diesel multiple units. In 1988 the service was handed over to the new Class '156' 'Sprinters' and these in turn will be replaced by 90 mph Class '158' 'Express' units waiting to go into service as this book is being prepared.

The line from Leicester through Coalville to Burton-on-Trent is another survivor. At present it is freight-only, but plans are slowly taking shape to re-introduce passenger traffic with a number of new stations along the route. Projected passenger services should commence in 1994-5 under the banner of the 'Ivanhoe Line' at an estimated cost of £12 million.

In the 1950s Leicester inhabitants enjoyed the choice of two main-line routes to London — the Great Central and the Midland — and both also crossed Northamptonshire. One could also get to London from Belgrave Road station via the East Coast Main Line to King's Cross, but this meant a slow journey to Grantham and then a change of trains, so it is debatable if anyone took this route. Today, Belgrave Road station and its line are long gone. Across the city, on the Great Central, the closure of the through route to Marylebone in 1966 had a significant impact on the railway scene in Leicester, and is still looked upon with sadness by many local folk who remember the sight of 'A3' 'Pacifics' on the top named trains, and later the Annesley to Woodford 'Windcutter' freight services rushing past with BR Standard '9F' 2-10-0s in charge. Leicester had lost its other direct link with Rugby in 1961 when the line through Countesthorpe and Broughton Astley, built by the Midland, closed completely.

Despite this apparent gloom and doom, there is still a great deal of railway interest to be seen in Leicestershire. The Midland Main Line is now experiencing a healthy increase in passenger traffic helped by the fast timings to London using HST sets. Part of the GC line is still alive with preserved steam and diesel-powered trains running from Loughborough to Belgrave and Birstall. There is also a second preserved steam line at Shackerstone on the former Nuneaton to Burton route.

Moving to Northamptonshire, although the total route mileage is not as large as Leicestershire, the volume of passenger traffic is substantial. Northampton itself has seen a rapid expansion over the last 20 years with new businesses moving to the area and the attendant increase in new housing development. Being only 65 miles from London, it is now a commuter town with frequent electric services to the capital, and the line is also of particular importance as it is often used as a diversionary route when the West Coast Main Line is closed between Roade and Rugby.

As with Leicestershire, the line closure that had the most impact on the county was the Great Central. Woodford Halse was a community that was reliant on the railway for its prosperity and employment; the area was dominated by the marshalling yards and the engine shed, its coaling tower once a landmark on the skyline. There was a constant background sound of shunting, train whistles, and passing trains virtually 24 hours a day. Now Woodford is without its railway and today the only sounds heard on the land that the lines used to occupy is the wind whistling through the trees and the calls of the farm animals.

Rail passengers in Northamptonshire have a choice of two main lines today — the West Coast and the Midland. The steel town of Corby, on the Kettering to Manton line, has very recently lost its passenger service after being restored for only a short time. Freight traffic still uses this line, avoiding the peak-hour bottleneck at Leicester.

Turning now to Cambridgeshire, we began to find that during the steam era it was a particularly under-photographed county. This was probably because much of the railway network consisted of meandering rural branch lines through flat fenland serving isolated villages. Train services were sparse and infrequent, which would not tempt photographers to venture to such out-of-the-way places. It is interesting to speculate whether the lines ever made a profit, so it is not surprising that many such routes disappeared under British Railways management. Many photographers concentrated their efforts on the East Coast Main Line at Peterborough which became part of Cambridgeshire after the county boundary changes in the 1970s. Huntingdon became part of Cambridgeshire at the same time, while Rutland merged with Leicestershire.

Cambridgeshire possessed one unique line that was often photographed — the Wisbech & Upwell Tramway. This was constructed to bring fruit and vegetables from market gardens south of Wisbech into the town for onward distribution, and much of the line ran alongside public roadways and had to be operated by specially constructed tram engines which required their wheels and motion to be covered with sideplates. The famous 'Toby the Tram Engine' in the 'Thomas the Tank Engine' books by the Rev W. Awdry was based on one of these engines, and dates from the time when the author was in charge of Emneth parish, near Wisbech.

To the south-west of Wisbech is March, which featured the enormous Whitemoor marshalling yard. Reduction in wagon-load traffic in favour of block trains spelled the end for this yard and it is now virtually unused. March also boasted an important locomotive depot with an allocation, on 1 January 1950, of 159 steam engines and five diesel shunters. Converted to diesel only in the early 1960s, this itself is now also closed.

Cambridge remains a busy station, not only with commuters but also visitors and the students of the many colleges. Services to London offer the choice of two destinations, King's Cross or Liverpool Street, the routes going their separate ways south of the city. Motive power has seen a number of changes in recent years. Following electrification, the Liverpool Street to Kings Lynn service was worked through to Cambridge by Class '86/2' electric locomotives and then diesel power onwards to Kings Lynn. In early 1989 this ceased, with diesel locomotives taking over for the whole journey from London. This through service was then withdrawn in May 1990. When the current electrification scheme is energised to Kings Lynn, electric power will take over once again.

The production of the 'present' photographs for this volume was not without its problems. We discovered bridges had been removed, cuttings filled in, and in extreme cases virtually no trace that a railway ever existed. It was a sad experience to discover how our once great railway heritage has been so decimated. Some of the most noticeable changes to the remaining lines have occurred within the last ten years — the Leicester re-signalling, the electrification of the East Coast Main Line and Cambridge routes, and the removal at various locations of goods yards and sidings once bustling with activity.

Considerable help and co-operation from many quarters was received to enable the present-day scenes to be recorded. Farmers allowed access to their private lands, house-owners allowed photographs from back gardens and at Bartlow we were graciously given a guided tour of the house and gardens that was once the station. Factory-owners also allowed us to visit their premises where they were built on old railway land, and the interest and enthusiasm that many had for our project was extremely encouraging. British Rail also supported our quest for obtaining the best photographs possible, for a number had to be taken on the 'wrong side of the fence'. On these occasions permission was granted and a railway official attended. Our thanks go to the Public Affairs Department at Stanier House, Birmingham, for their assistance and patience!

A special word of thanks must go to the photographers who provided the 'past' material, without which the book could not have been produced. The excellence of their work is here for all to see.

Our wives and families have had to endure many hours of solitude while we studied maps and photographs and then went out 'on location'. The sight of Chris Milner boldly going where no man has gone for a long time into dense undergrowth armed with a camera, *convinced that a railway was once there*, will long be remembered. The writing involved long hours locked away in a room with reference material scattered all round, usually with the music of Vivaldi or Bach playing as a background.

We think that all the effort has been worth it. The hope is that you enjoy reading this book as much as we have enjoyed producing it, and that it re-kindles memories of a bygone railway age.

Chris Milner
Earl Shilton

Chris Banks
Hinckley

9

LEICESTERSHIRE

LEICESTER LONDON ROAD (1): London Road station opened in 1892 as part of the Midland Railway's improvements, replacing the earlier Campbell Street station which had become inadequate for the growing traffic. The overall roof lost its glass during the Second World War and was never replaced. Looking north, ex-LNER 'V2' 2-6-2 No 60963 (York based) runs into platform 3 past the East signal box positioned on the platform. This rare visitor would have looked more at home at the other main-line station, Leicester Central, but on this occasion, Tuesday 4 May 1965, it was on a Newcastle–South Coast Saga Special for old age pensioners, and came off the train at Leicester to be replaced by diesel power. No 60963 had entered traffic in January 1943 at Gateshead and this was almost certainly its last appearance at Leicester for it was withdrawn from York on the 29th of the next month. *Gerald Morgan*

Taken from the same position on 25 August 1990, double-heading the 10.40 Yarmouth to Birmingham New Street are Class '31' Nos 31147 and 31462. Notice the 'Welcome to Leicester' signs in various languages, reflecting the cosmopolitan population of the city today.

LEICESTER LONDON ROAD (2): 'Jubilee' '6P' 4-6-0 No 45659 *Drake* runs into Leicester under Swain Street bridge on the 12 noon Bradford to St Pancras express on Tuesday 9 August 1960. Note the train-spotters perched precariously on the middle girders of the bridge. *Drake* dated back to December 1934, went new to Leeds Holbeck, and was withdrawn in May 1963 from the same depot. *Barry O. Hilton*

Swain Street bridge remains, now much more attractive in brighter paint, but the signals have disappeared along with the water column. Also, the goods shed, to the left of the 1960 photograph, has been demolished. The 10.40 Yarmouth to Birmingham runs in with Class '31' Nos 31545 and 31178 in charge on 11 August 1990. This train was popular with photographers as it usually produced this motive power.

LEICESTER LONDON ROAD (3): Looking north from the end of platform 2 at London Road on 30 March 1969 with preserved ex-LNER 'A3' 4-6-2 No 4472 *Flying Scotsman* running in on a Flying Scotsman Enterprises railtour to St Pancras. This engine was no stranger to the city for in May 1950 as No 60103 it was transferred to Leicester Central shed where it remained until December 1953, then going on to Grantham. Dominating the scene in the background of this photograph is the coaling tower of Leicester Midland depot, soon to be demolished. *P.N. Clay*

The same scene on 3 June 1986 shows the signals and layout still intact, but today all have been replaced by the new Leicester power signalling box brought into use in 1987. The train is the 13.30 Norwich to Birmingham New Street powered by Class '31' No 31418. This service is no longer locomotive-hauled, being worked nowadays by the new-generation Class '158' 'Express' units.

LEICESTER MIDLAND DEPOT was situated just north of the station on the up side. The first shed was erected soon after the Midland Counties line opened through Leicester in 1840, and various additions and alterations were made right through until 1900. For the next 40 years the collection of fast-decaying buildings remained until a start was made in 1944 to remedy this unsatisfactory situation. This resulted in a complete rebuild in the form of a new concrete roundhouse with ashplant and coaling tower. Leicester was an important depot and on 1 January 1949 the allocation was 75 locomotives. This view was recorded on Sunday 2 September 1962 with over 30 locomotives on view in the yard, including Nos 41225, 41279, 42331, 42334, 42338, 43969, 44030, 44231, 44932, 45264, 46113, 48640, 70010, 70013, 75042, 75059, 92103, 92111 and 92120. Such a large collection in the yard was unusual, and was due to the roundhouse turntable being out of use for repair. *Horace A. Gamble*

The same scene on a Sunday in February 1989 shows that the only visible occupant of the yard is a permanent way track machine, while a St Pancras to Sheffield HST passes in the background. The depot closed to steam traction on 13 June 1966 and the roundhouse was demolished in 1970. The yard is now used as a diesel stabling point.

LEICESTER CENTRAL: We now move to the other main-line station, Leicester Central. The Great Central arrived late in the railway age, not opening for through traffic until 9 March 1899. This view, on Saturday 16 August 1958, shows Colwick-based 'K2' 2-6-0 No 61753 on an up local. In the background are ex-GWR 'Hall' Class 4-6-0s Nos 4970 *Sketty Hall*, Taunton-based, and 5916 *Trinity Hall*, Oxley-based. The presence of GWR engines was a regular feature at summer weekends, having worked up from Oxford or Banbury on through trains from Bournemouth to the north. *Barry O. Hilton*

Another view at the south end of the station on Saturday 16 June 1962. Waiting for work is 'Royal Scot' '7P' 4-6-0 No 46106, formerly named *Gordon Highlander* (the nameplates had been removed earlier in the year) and bearing a 15E shedplate, which was the code of Leicester Central depot at that time. Most of the 'Scots' transferred to the Central were throwouts from other parts of the system and were in poor mechanical condition. No 46106 here looks the exception, and has even been cleaned by the shed staff. This was the only member of the class to be fitted with BR standard smoke deflectors, and was transferred to Central shed in May 1962 replacing withdrawn 'B1' 4-6-0s. Its regular working, shared with classmate No 46118, was on the afternoon York to Bournemouth between Leicester and Banbury, returning on a Woodford Halse to Leicester local. Officially 'on loan' to Leicester, its time on the Central was short for with No 46118 it was transferred to Carlisle Upperby at the end of June, where it remained until withdrawal in December the same year. *Horace A. Gamble*

Through passenger services between Nottingham and Marylebone were withdrawn on 5 September 1966, and a service of six trains each way between Rugby Central and Nottingham operated with diesel multiple units was the replacement. Leicester Central became what was probably the largest unstaffed halt in the country, with tickets issued on the trains. Actually, the station was still 'staffed' by one lady who ran W.H. Smith's bookstall on the platform, which remained open on a trial basis. The station closed completely on 5 May 1969, although the last services ran on 3 May. This was the scene on 30 September 1988, the link with the past being the factory in the background.

LEICESTER SOUTH GOODS yard and warehouse, with the carriage sheds on the far left. This is a mid-1950s scene when the Great Central was alive and well. *David W. Webb*

On 30 September 1988 the goods yard is in use as Vic Berry's now famous scrapyard. The warehouse in the background still remains. If current plans come to fruition this scene will again change, for Leicester City Council is looking to acquire the land for redevelopment as light industrial and retail units, office accommodation, and a number of flats and houses. Plans have been submitted for Vic Berry and his company to move its operations to a new 117-acre rail-connected site near Desford, 7 miles out from the city centre. However, the future is now somewhat uncertain, following a devastating fire in the early hours of 10 March 1991, which gutted over 130 railway carriages.

LEICESTER SOUTH GOODS signal box with the Great Central engine depot in the background. The date is Tuesday 23 April 1957 and York-based 'V2' 2-6-2 No 60864 is having an easy time on the goods line with a down freight. The 'V2' was withdrawn on 16 March 1964 still on allocation at York. The Central engine shed was a relatively small establishment, but was nevertheless an important depot strategically placed for engine and crew changing and had a number of local turns as well as long-distance top link duties. The allocation on 1 January 1949 was 27 locomotives, all ex-LNER types: 17 'B1' 4-6-0s, 6 'J2' 0-6-0s, 1 'J1' 0-6-0, 1 'J5' 0-6-0, 1 'J11' 0-6-0 and 1 'J69' 0-6-0T. Transfer to LMR control took place on 23 February 1958 with a code change from 38C to 15E, the allocation on that day being 20 locomotives. Closure took place on Saturday 11 July 1964, the final allocation being six Stanier 4-6-0s (44847, 44848, 44984, 45221, 45342 and 45416) which all went to Annesley, and one diesel shunter, D3785, which was transferred to Leicester Midland. *Barry O. Hilton*

The trackbed is now a footpath, Great Central Way. There is still a railway presence, for hidden behind the hedge is the line leading to Vic Berry's yard from the Leicester to Burton line. 30 September 1988.

MARLOW ROAD BRIDGE: An up freight bound for Woodford Halse approaches Marlow Road bridge in the Leicester suburbs on Saturday 23 March 1957. Standard '9F' 2-10-0 No 92068 is the locomotive, a type that revolutionised the freight workings on this route. Built at Crewe, No 92068 entered traffic on 29 December 1955 and was first allocated to Doncaster. Withdrawal came in January 1966 from Derby shed. *Barry O. Hilton*

The scene on 18 September 1988 is again part of the Great Central Way footpath. The cutting is filled in up to the top of the bridge parapet in the background of the 1957 photograph, the original brick piers now buried underneath.

LEICESTER BELGRAVE ROAD: This was the Great Northern Railway terminus in the city, opened on 1 January 1883. Situated $3/4$ mile from the city centre, it was an impressive building with five platforms covered by a twin arched roof. It served a route that left the Welham Junction to Grantham line at Marefield Junction and provided through trains to Grantham, connecting with trains to King's Cross. The train service was sparse and underused and it came as no surprise when the line closed to passenger traffic after the departure of the 18.10 to Melton Mowbray on 5 December 1953, hauled by 'J6' 0-6-0 No 64225. It left 2 minutes late, preceded by the usual ringing of a handbell. The station was, however, still used after this date for weekend excursion traffic to Skegness and Mablethorpe, and this view shows Colwick 'B1' 4-6-0 No 61092 leaving on a Saturday special to the East Coast in the summer of 1960. The last time an excursion left the station was in September 1962, but freight continued to run down the branch until 29 May 1964. A chord line connecting the goods warehouse to the Midland line at Humberstone was constructed, but this was taken out of use in May 1967. The station was demolished in 1972 and the warehouse lasted in private hands until 1985. *David W. Webb*

On 25 August 1990, a block of flats now hides the Belgrave Road station site, which is occupied by a supermarket. No evidence can now be found that a railway ever existed.

Leicester to Market Harborough

WELFORD ROAD BRIDGE, about a mile south of London Road station, forms the backdrop for this view as Beyer-Garratt 2-6-6-2T No 47999, with fixed coal bunker, leaves for the south. The date is Saturday 12 March 1955 and this impressive locomotive had not long to run, being withdrawn in January 1956 from Toton. *M. Mason*

By 1990 rationalisation had taken place for only two lines now run under the bridge. The former freight lines which ran over to the right of this scene were lifted in 1989. 'Sprinter' set No 150131 runs past on the 13.50 Nottingham to Coventry on 10 July 1990.

KNIGHTON TUNNEL had two portals for the freight lines and main passenger lines. 1925-built '4P' 4-4-0 No 41103 leaves on the up main line with a semi-fast to Bedford on Thursday 26 August 1954. Withdrawal for this engine came in November 1957 from Derby shed. *M. Mason*

On 10 July 1990, the signals have gone and the second tunnel bore is now trackless. HST power car No 43049 heads the 13.28 Sheffield to St Pancras.

KNIGHTON SOUTH JUNCTION on Monday 18 May 1964, the junction for the line to Burton and Coalville. Stanier '5MT' 4-6-0 No 45289 passes on a Leicester to Bromford Bridge, Birmingham, race special. *Horace A. Gamble*

By 25 June 1986 little change had taken place, but today all has changed, for four days later the new Leicester power box was brought into use and the semaphore signals made redundant. Class '45/1' No 45137, also now a memory, hauls the Chipmans weed-killing train down the main line towards Market Harborough.

WIGSTON MAGNA was the first station south from Leicester on the main line, and was one of three stations at Wigston. This view was recorded on Saturday 4 March 1961 with LMS '4F' 0-6-0 No 44575 running in for its scheduled stop with the 07.02 Wellingborough to Leicester local. This 0-6-0 ended its days at Coalville, withdrawal coming in November 1964. *Mike Mitchell*

The station closed on 1 January 1968. On 10 July 1990 the scene is greatly changed, with the station gone and the main line now just double track. HST power cars Nos 43152 at the head and 43057 at the rear speed past on the 07.30 St Pancras to Nottingham.

KIBWORTH NORTH with Standard '9F' 2-10-0 No 92095 going well on an up freight. The date is Saturday 17 August 1963. Note the lovely Midland signals visible through the bridge arch. *Barry O. Hilton*

On Sunday 21 May 1989, Class '20' Nos 20228+20145 run past Kibworth on a 12.55 Leicester to St Pancras special as part of an InterCity 'Diesel Day' organised by Hertfordshire Railtours. The bridge remains, but the signal box and signals together with the goods loop have gone.

MARKET HARBOROUGH: Class '40' No D268 runs into Market Harborough station and takes the Rugby line with a mixed train from Peterborough on Saturday 28 May 1966. The line closed one week later on 6 June, freight services having been withdrawn in April 1965. The original 'main line' when built by the London & Birmingham Railway was from Rugby to a junction with the Midland at Luffenham on the line through Stamford to Peterborough, which opened as a single track to Market Harborough on 1 May 1850. Eventually becoming LNWR property and by then double track, the route was used for through Birmingham to Yarmouth trains. On closure day, the last train into Rugby, the 20.12 from Peterborough, was formed of four coaches powered by Class '24' No D5085. *Barry O. Hilton*

HST power car No 43122 passes through Market Harborough station on the 12.28 Sheffield to St Pancras on 4 June 1990. The brick goods shed on the right still stands and the down platform has been extended for the 'InterCity 125' trains. The trackbed is being used to construct a new car park.

MARKET HARBOROUGH had its own motive power depot and this view on Sunday 12 March 1961 has '4F' 0-6-0s and a Stanier '8F' 2-8-0 on shed. A small two-road establishment with a 65,000-gallon water tank as its roof, it dated back to around 1899 and was of LNWR origin. The depot was a sub-shed to Rugby and in October 1955 was granted its own code of 2F. This changed to 15F in February 1958, but two years later reverted to sub-shed status again, this time under Leicester Midland. The allocation was usually around six locomotives, but visitors at weekends swelled the available locomotives. A visit to the shed on Sunday 21 February 1954 found the following engines present: 42576 (2A), 42577 (2A), 44214 (17A), 44231 (15C), 44395 (2A), 45493 (2A), 48122 (2A), 48173 (2A), 48440 (1A), 48559 (2A), 49415 (2A) and 58269 (2A). (1A: Willesden, 2A: Rugby, 15C: Leicester Midland, 17A: Derby) The depot closed on 4 October 1965. *K.C.H. Fairey*

The motive power depot site is occupied by a storage tank for the Tungsten Batteries factory in this 4 June 1990 view. Perhaps if you dug down a little way into the ground you would find some buried ash as an epitaph to the engines and men that worked from this friendly little depot.

Leicester to Birmingham line

WIGSTON NORTH JUNCTION: We now return to Wigston to examine the Leicester to Nuneaton and Birmingham line as far as Hinckley. Opened as a through route in 1864, the section through Leicestershire was LNWR property over which the Midland had running rights. The line left the Midland main line at Wigston North Junction and curved round to Wigston Glen Parva. Standard '2MT' 2-6-0 No 78020 takes this section of line with the 17.55 Leicester to Nuneaton Trent Valley local on Saturday 22 August 1959. *Michael Mensing*

The scene nowadays boasts a very successful new station known as South Wigston, opened on 10 May 1986. This is the Birmingham-side platform — the Leicester-side is just behind the photographer. Passing by is Class '56' No 56078 on a Bow (East London) to Croft (via Cambridge and Peterborough) granite train, on 2 June 1989.

WIGSTON GLEN PARVA (1): The view from the road overbridge just east of Wigston Glen Parva station recorded on Saturday 27 June 1959. The 16.30 Leicester London Road to Birmingham New Street runs through, composed of a Birmingham RCW three-car Class '104' set, then only two years old. Much older is the ex-LNWR 0-8-0 in the background standing on the south curve line waiting to follow on with a Nuneaton-bound goods. *Michael Mensing*

A new-generation 'Sprinter' set, No 156409, on a Norwich to Birmingham working, passes the same spot on 3 September 1988. In the left background can be seen the new platforms of South Wigston station.

WIGSTON GLEN PARVA (2): Looking in the opposite direction on Saturday 8 June 1963, Standard '9F' 2-10-0 No 92101 shuffles through on a mixed freight heading for Leicester. This engine came to Leicester Midland shed in March 1958 and, except for a couple of months at Wellingborough in 1960, remained at Leicester until April 1965 when transfer to Birkenhead took place. Glen Parva station closed on 4 March 1968. Note the gas lamps on the platforms, which remained in use right through to closure. *Mike Mitchell*

On Tuesday 31 May 1988 nothing remains of the station, and trees and grass have taken over from neatly tended station gardens. Glen Parva station buildings were of a modest nature and constructed of wood; they disappeared soon after closure. Even the telegraph poles have gone, their wires now ducted underground. First-generation 'Sprinter' set No 150128 runs past on a Coventry to Nottingham working, few if any of the passengers realising that a station ever existed here.

CROFT station opened around 1879 and was a direct result of the granite workings which created work in the village. The station closed on 4 March 1968. This view taken shortly before closure, shows a Cravens two-car DMU leaving on a Nuneaton Trent Valley to Leicester service. *Barry O. Hilton*

On 21 June 1991, the 13.25 Birmingham New Street–Harwich Parkeston Quay passes Croft station site. In the background are the ECC quarries sidings, with their distinctive freight wagons. Plans are now at an early stage for the re-opening of a station.

HINCKLEY: The line to Leicester from Nuneaton opened as far as Hinckley on 1 January 1862. This is the station on 26 August 1974 looking towards Leicester with the 15.28 Birmingham to Cambridge just setting off. The train is composed of a three-car Birmingham RCW Class '104' set at the rear and, leading, a Swindon-built Class '120' 'Cross Country' unit. *Michael Mensing*

By 31 May 1988, the former vantage point, the footbridge linking the platforms, has been removed, but otherwise little has changed from the 1974 view, other than the new pedestrian footbridge which has replaced the much older plated steel example. The train is Tyseley set No T227, a Class '114' two-car DMU Nos 53019 and 54027, dating back to 1956. Although the rear blind shows Lincoln (coincidentally this unit's first allocation when new) it is really the 17.11 Birmingham to Nottingham.

Leicester to Rugby line

This was the original Midland Counties Railway route to London via Rugby opened on 30 June 1840, but on the opening of the Midland direct line to St Pancras in 1868 it was demoted to a branch line. On the last day of operation, 30 December 1961, the morning services were operated by '4MT' 2-6-4T No 42062 and '2MT' 2-6-0 No 46446, both Rugby engines. The afternoon workings were by DMU. A four-coach special organised by the Leicester Railway Society, hauled by 2-6-4T No 42331, ran during the afternoon through sub-zero temperatures and snow. The evening trains were worked once again by 46446 and 42062, the 2-6-4T taking the last train of all, the 19.28 Rugby to Leicester and 21.40 return. The line officially closed on 1 January 1962. After this it was used for wagon storage, and demolition and lifting of tracks did not commence until 1964.

WIGSTON SOUTH: The first station out from Leicester was Wigston South and this view, dated Saturday 22 July 1961, has Stanier 2-6-4T No 42573 on the 10.17 Rugby to Leicester. Note the delivery boy waiting at the crossing gates, and all the railway fitments from a bygone age. *Mike Mitchell*

On 4 June 1990 the land is occupied by a factory and its car park. Behind the photographer, on the site of the down staggered platform, is the South Wigston Health Centre.

COUNTESTHORPE was the next station along the line, seen here in 1957 with ex-LNWR '7F' 0-8-0 No 49094 on a southbound freight. Note the staggered platforms, which were a feature of stations along this route as well as the numerous level crossings. The 0-8-0 survived longer than the line, being withdrawn from Bletchley shed in November 1962. *David W. Webb*

Countesthorpe station site is now occupied by a modern housing estate, its residents commuting into Leicester on ever increasingly congested roads. On 4 June 1990 there is no evidence that a railway ever passed this way.

BROUGHTON ASTLEY, 10 miles out from Leicester, looking towards Rugby. The station house had been rebuilt from an existing one and had a local reputation for being haunted. The date of this view is Thursday 21 September 1961, and Fowler '4MT' 2-6-4T No 42352 heads the 16.28 from Rugby to Leicester. This engine lasted until May 1962, Leicester Midland being its last home. *Michael Mensing*

The same view on 22 June 1991; close inspection revealed that part of the platform edge has survived, but apart from that the site is very overgrown and is rapidly returning to nature.

Great Central south of Leicester

AYLESTONE: Monday 15 August 1966, and the quiet of a summer evening is momentarily broken. On the way out from Leicester is Colwick-based Stanier '5MT' 4-6-0 No 45267 on the early evening departure from Nottingham Victoria to Marylebone, crossing the Grand Union canal. No 45267 was transferred to Wigan Springs Branch in November 1966, only a week before Colwick shed closed, and remained there until withdrawal during the week ending 14 October 1967. *Horace A. Gamble*

Trees and undergrowth are taking over on 25 August 1990. The former railway bridge still crosses the canal and is used as part of the Great Central Way footpath. The attractive wooden bridge on the left of the 1966 photograph is now replaced by a concrete version

ASHBY MAGNA (1): The station on Thursday 21 September 1961, looking south, as the experimental English Electric gas turbine locomotive GT3 runs through on a test train. The engine was designed specifically to look like a steam locomotive and, as the manufacturers had their factory at Whetstone, it was convenient to base it at Leicester Central shed. It disappeared from active use in February 1963 and was eventually cut up at T.W. Ward's yard at Brindle Heath, Manchester, in March 1966. *Michael Mensing*

The station site on 11 September 1988 shows that the M1 motorway has been the winner in the transport stakes, running parallel to the old trackbed.

ASHBY MAGNA (2): Just south of the station was a short tunnel, more like a covered-over cutting than a true tunnel piercing a hillside. This is the location on Saturday 29 August 1959 for a portrait of 'K3' 2-6-0 No 61838 on a Newcastle to Cardiff express. Built in January 1925 as LNER No 127, this 'K3' lasted until March 1960, its last home being Woodford Halse which was then part of the LMR. *Barry O. Hilton*

Revisited on 11 May 1989, the tunnel was found to be still in use, but now only for storage purposes by a local farmer. The steep cutting and old trackbed leading up to it are now being taken over by nature.

LUTTERWORTH, with Standard '5MT' 4-6-0 No 73004 leaving on the 14.38 Marylebone to Nottingham Victoria on Saturday 22 May 1965. The station is in the background, with the new M1 motorway over to the left. The days of the Central were by now numbered, with just over a year to run before the line was severed south of Rugby. Lutterworth saw its last trains on 3 May 1969. No 73004 had an association with Leicestershire for it had gone new to Leicester Midland shed in June 1951 and remained on allocation there until May 1958. When this scene was recorded it was based at Nuneaton, and had no doubt been borrowed by Annesley in place of a failed locomotive. It moved on the following week to Wrexham Croes Newydd; final withdrawal came from Bolton in October 1967. *Michael Mensing*

On 11 May 1989 an industrial unit occupies the trackbed and the area is permeated with the constant background noise of an increasingly congested M1 motorway.

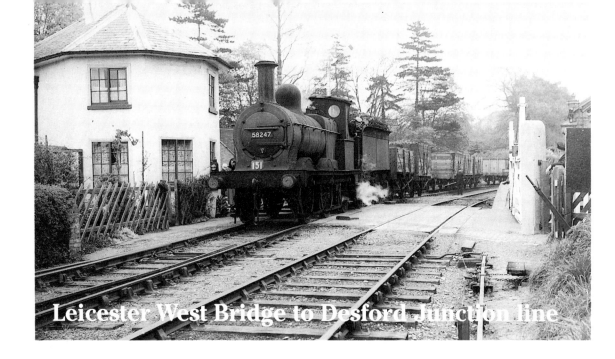

GLENFIELD: The former Leicester to Swannington line opened from Leicester to Bagworth on 17 July 1832 and throughout in November 1833, being one of the earliest lines to operate in the country. This scene is at Glenfield with Coalville-based Midland '2F' 0-6-0 No 58247 playing with some wagons and holding up traffic over the crossing in around 1951. Just a little further up the line behind the wagons is the 1 mile 36 yard Glenfield tunnel; it was built to sub-standard clearances which meant that only the Midland '2F' 0-6-0s could get through, ensuring that they lasted well into the 1960s. When they were simply too old to perform their duties, two Standard 2MT 2-6-0s (Nos 78013 and 78028) were drafted in to work the line after having their cabs and tender fronts cut down. Even then clearances in the tunnel were in inches! The last time a '2F' worked the line was on 14 December 1963 on the 05.48 Desford Junction to West Bridge and 12.15 return, the engine involved being No 58148. Passenger services were withdrawn from the line on 24 September 1928 and final closure came on 24 April 1966. Glenfield tunnel was sold to Leicester Corporation for £5 in 1969 and is now sealed up at both ends. *John F. Clay*

In April 1989 the only link with the earlier photograph is the tall trees in the background. The site is now occupied by warden-controlled homes for the elderly and part of the trackbed is a footpath to nearby Ratby. There is one other clue, for the road is called Stephenson Court after the builder of the line.

RATBY, the next station along the line, was of wooden construction and lasted into the 1960s, slowly rotting away. Midland '2F' 0-6-0 No 58163 crosses the main street at Ratby in 1959 with a train for West Bridge. This engine finished its days at Coalville, being withdrawn in October 1961. *Chris Banks*

Today no trace of the railway exists other than a narrow pathway which is all that remains of the trackbed. A reminder that a railway once existed is 'The Railway Inn' which stands alongside the footpath and sports a pub sign showing a GWR 'King' Class 4-6-0. More appropriate would have been a humble '2F' 0-6-0!

Leicester to Coalville line

The Knighton Junction, Leicester, to Desford section of this line opened on 1 August 1849. It carried passenger traffic until 7 September 1964, but still carries freight today and plans are under consideration to re-open to passengers with a number of new stations. Indeed, passenger trains still use the line, but only as specials to Coalville when the Mantle Lane freight depot stages its annual Open Day, held for the last time in May 1991.

DESFORD: This view, on Saturday 14 September 1963, is at Desford level crossing with '2F' 0-6-0 No 58182 returning to Coalville light engine. This was the very last active Midland '2F' and it performed its last duties on Wednesday 18 December 1963 as yard pilot at Coalville. *Barry O. Hilton*
  Desford Crossing on 21 June 1991, now relegated to a single line, but on the right-hand side of the photograph is the old station house, now a private residence. Just beyond the crossing is the proposed site for the new station platform.

BARDON HILL SIDINGS between Desford and Coalville on Saturday 5 June 1965, as Coalville-based Stanier '8F' 2-8-0 No 48552 heads for home on coal empties. Note the ancient Midland signal. *Horace A. Gamble*

Tyseley Class '116' DMU set No 324 (53053+59672+53101) passes Bardon Hill signal box on the 14.46 Leicester to Burton special. The date is 3 June 1990, Coalville Mantle Lane open day.

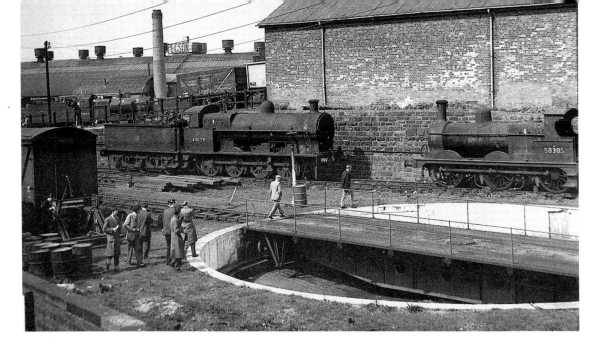

COALVILLE TOWN (1): There had been some sort of engine depot at Coalville from the earliest days of the line; records show that a three-road brick engine shed, with coal stage and turntable, opened in 1890 replacing an earlier building, and it was this building that remained in use into British Railways days, situated on the west side of Coalville Town station. This view of the shed yard was recorded during a Leicester Railway Society visit on Saturday 27 May 1961. Nuneaton-based ex-LNWR 0-8-0 No 49079 is visible together with 'at home' '2F' 0-6-0 No 58305. Coded 17C, 15D and finally 15E under British Railways, Coalville closed on 4 October 1965 but remained as a stabling point for around ten Type 2 diesels. The final allocation on closure day consisted of 13 Stanier '8F' 2-8-0s (48137, 48219, 48376, 48380, 48388, 48467, 48552, 48617, 48619, 48644, 48687, 48696 and 48699). None were withdrawn, all being transferred away, seven going to Leicester Midland and six to Westhouses. *Horace A. Gamble*

On 3 June 1990 the shed site has been taken over by industrial units. Just recognisable is the Pegsons factory in the background, engaged in the production of quarry equipment.

COALVILLE TOWN (2): The station in 1956, as the 13.55 Burton to Leicester arrives hauled by Derby-based '2P' 4-4-0 No 40407. On leaving the station the train would cross the busy A50 road by a level crossing controlled by an unusually high Midland signal box which remained in use until 1985 when it was removed for preservation. *Ken Hunt*

The site of Coalville Town station again on the last Open Day, 26 May 1991. Open days had been held at Coalville since 1978, initially attracting around 3,000 people. This had increased to over 15,000 on the last day, and more than £90,000 had been raised over the years for local charities, but now the sidings and train crew facilities at Mantle Lane are closed. This photograph shows Class '60' Nos 60057 *Adam Smith* and 60032 *William Booth* heading a 'Pathfinder' tour from Ayr to Bristol, which included a visit to the open day on its itinerary. It was running 3 hours late due to an earlier tour not keeping to schedule and causing chaos to the single line working.

SWANNINGTON CROSSING, just north of Coalville, in 1957. Ivatt '2MT' 2-6-0 No 46447 runs over on a Burton to Leicester stopping train. A station was provided here just on the other side of the crossing, but this closed on 18 June 1951. *Ken Hunt*

By Sunday 3 June 1990 the line is single track with the signal box and crossing gates gone; automatic barriers now control the traffic. Borrowed by Tyseley is Longsight Class '108' DMU set No 260 (51905+54488) on the 14.00 Derby to Coalville special.

Burton to Nuneaton line

SHACKERSTONE: Opened on 1 September 1873, this was a joint LNWR and Midland venture built to tap the coalfields of north-west Leicestershire and over into the Derbyshire workings around Swadlincote. This is Shackerstone station where a junction existed for the double-track 'main' line through to Burton via Measham and a single-track branch through to Coalville. This was the only station on the joint line to have a footbridge, necessitated by a public footpath crossing the railway at this point. On the down platform there was a slight rise in the platform face alongside the station buildings, a modification carried out in 1906 for the arrival of King Edward VII who was visiting nearby Gopsal Hall, to assist the King in stepping down from the train. It sadly failed, for when the train arrived and the Royal coach stopped at this special part of the platform, it was discovered that there had been a miscalculation in the height. The door would not open — the platform was too high! Passenger services were withdrawn as early as 12 April 1931, but freight trains continued to use the line until 1970. This view, recorded around 1957, shows Stanier '8F' 2-8-0 No 48286 coming off the Measham line with empties for Nuneaton. *Ken Hunt*

Today Shackerstone station is still alive, for it is the home of the Shackerstone Railway Society Ltd. Steam-hauled trains run the 2^1/$_2$ miles to Market Bosworth, and a further 1^3/$_4$-mile extension to Shenton is nearing completion and awaiting official opening to passengers.

MARKET BOSWORTH station, with Ivatt '2MT' 2-6-2T No 41321 on a Leicester Railway Society 21st Anniversary Special on Saturday 27 May 1961. The train consisted of a three-coach push-and-pull set of ex-LMS stock, and had covered many of the Leicestershire lines not open to passenger traffic. This part of the tour had covered the line from Shepshed, through Shackerstone Junction, and on to Nuneaton with stops for photographs along the way. This view is looking south towards Nuneaton. *John F. Clay*

On Sunday 30 July 1989 Bagnall 0-4-0ST *Linda*, built in 1941, runs round its train to return to Shackerstone. The train contained an old Park Royal-built ex-diesel multiple unit coach used as an observation car. The station building still stands and is in use as a car repair garage.

Midland Main Line north of Leicester

LOUGHBOROUGH MIDLAND on Sunday 6 July 1975. Approaching the station from the north is the 09.50 Nottingham to St Pancras with Class '45' No 45144 in charge. Over to the right is the Brush Engineering Works with its falcon emblem proudly standing on the roof. The impressive Midland goods shed dominates the yard to the left. *Tom Heavyside*

Photographed from the same position (the station footbridge) on 28 July 1990 is the Saturdays-only 09.55 Loughborough ARC Depot to Ardingley, near Haywards Heath, stone train. Motive power is Class '56' No 56105. The goods shed and signal box have now gone, but the yard is still in use. The Brush falcon also appears to have flown!

HATHERN: The village of Hathern, 5 miles north of Loughborough, was situated in Leicestershire, but prospective rail travellers had to cross into Nottinghamshire to catch their trains, for the station, which closed on 4 January 1960, was just over the county border. This view, in 1958, shows Standard '5MT' 4-6-0 No 73138, with Caprotti valve gear, approaching the station on an up express. Hathern stoneworks forms the background. *Ken Hunt*

By 15 August 1990, the old stoneworks buildings have been converted into separate industrial units. The left-hand embankment is now much more overgrown as the 12.28 Sheffield to St Pancras speeds past with power car No 43102 at the front end.

KEGWORTH: Like Hathern, Kegworth, a few miles further north, was in Leicestershire but the station was in Nottinghamshire. Stanier '8F' 2-8-0 No 48638, Toton-based, runs past the station in 1958 with a southbound coal train on the freight lines. Kegworth remained open until 4 March 1968, while the '8F' remained active until January 1966, its last home shed being Westhouses. *Ken Hunt*

On 15 August 1990 Class '156' 'Sprinter' No 156418 passes on the 08.54 Liverpool Lime Street to Norwich on the up main. No evidence of a station now exists.

Great Central north of Leicester

BELGRAVE AND BIRSTALL station, 5 miles north of Leicester city centre. The date is Saturday 11 May 1963 and the Central line is host to 'Jubilee' 4-6-0 No 45658 *Keyes*, Leeds Holbeck-based, on an up Rugby League Cup Final special. The station had already closed by this time, on 4 March 1963, but still looks in a good state of repair. *Barry O. Hilton*

Since this June 1989 photograph was taken, trains are again running here, for track has been relaid from Rothley to form an extension to the preserved Great Central Railway from Loughborough, and the station has been re-named Leicester North. Comparing the two photographs will show that the lineside footpath has been altered, but the bridge in the background leading to the Golf Club still stands and the platform can still be discerned.

KINCHLEY LANE, between Quorn and Rothley, in 1950. Ex-LNER 'B1' 4-6-0 No 61159, Gorton-based, passes by on a Manchester to Marylebone express. This engine had been new to traffic in May 1947 and had started its career at this Manchester depot, but had a very short life, for withdrawal came on 24 September 1963 at Immingham. *John F. Clay*

The line on 15 August 1990 is single track, but plans are being formulated to return this part of the old Great Central to double track after a large injection of cash into the company. Ex-GWR '5700' Class 0-6-0PT No 7760, on loan from Tyseley Railway Museum, heads the 13.45 Loughborough to Rothley.

North Leicestershire

MELTON MOWBRAY is the home of pork-pies, and a centre for foxhunting and Stilton cheese. This is the North station which was situated on the ex-Great Northern and LNWR joint line that ran from Welham Junction on the LNWR line north of Market Harborough to Stathern Junction. Here it split into two lines, one going to Saxondale Junction and the other to Bottesford, both on the GNR Nottingham to Grantham route. South of Melton the Leicester Belgrave Road branch joined at Marefield Junction. The line opened throughout in December 1879, and although passenger services were withdrawn on 7 December 1953, continued use was made of the line for excursion traffic until 1962. The last freight train ran from Melton North to Colwick on 7 September 1964, thus effectively closing the line from this date. This view of North station was recorded on 8 July 1962: 'B1' Class 4-6-0 No 61361 leaves on the 10.10 Leicester Belgrave Road to Skegness. *P.H. Wells*

On 3 September 1988 there is no evidence that a railway ever ran this way, for the area is now occupied by an industrial estate.

MELTON JUNCTION on the Midland line at Melton Mowbray, with the GNR/LNWR joint line crossing over in the background. This is the junction of the lines from Syston and Nottingham; the section from Syston, on the Midland main line from Leicester, opened to Melton on 1 September 1846. The route from Stamford to Peterborough opened on 2 October the same year, but due to opposition by a local landowner Melton was not connected to Stamford until 1 May 1848. Here '2P' 4-4-0 No 40542 and an unidentified 'Jubilee' 4-6-0 come off the Nottingham line with an express that would take the route through Manton Junction to St Pancras. The scene was recorded in July 1958. *P.H. Groom*

On 8 March 1984 Class '56' No 56063 comes along the Syston line with a Mountsorrel to Radlett Redland company train. Passenger services were withdrawn from the Nottingham line in 1966, having commenced on 2 February 1880, but the line still remains in place and is used as the Old Dalby test track for the BR Derby Technical Centre. When the Vale of Belvoir coalfield begins production in 1991 it will be used for coal trains once again. Since this photograph was taken, a DIY store has been built in the field to the left.

MELTON MOWBRAY TOWN (1): The station can be seen in the background of this photograph as Fowler 2-6-4T No 42339 makes a rousing start with a local to Nottingham in April 1957, before the days of diesel multiple units operating in any great numbers. No 42339 was withdrawn in September 1963 from Bolton shed after giving 34 years service. *P.H. Groom*

The Corby to Lackenby steel empties leaves Melton on 10 July 1990 with Class '37' Nos 37502 *British Steel Teesside* and 37501 *Teesside Steelmaster* in charge. Class '60' locomotives have now taken over this service. Because of the growth of foliage since the 1957 photograph was recorded, it was not possible to stand in exactly the same position.

54

MELTON MOWBRAY TOWN (2): The station opened in 1846 and still serves the town today. This view looking west in 1956 has Stanier '8F' 2-8-0 No 48305 braving the cold with a Kettering-bound freight. This engine ended its working life at Speke Junction in January 1968, going on to Barry scrapyard in September. It was rescued for preservation in November 1985 by the Great Central Railway and is presently awaiting restoration. *H.N. James*

On 3 September 1988 Class '47' No 47417, originally one of the first batch to be built and numbered D1516, runs into Melton on the ten-coach 07.50 Birmingham New Street to Yarmouth.

SAXBY JUNCTION, 5 miles east of Melton Mowbray. It was here that the local landowner Lord Harborough opposed the railway so fiercely that it had to take a different route from the one surveyed, resulting in a severe curve in the track. This caused a problem when the route came to be used by Midland expresses from Nottingham and in 1892 by mutual agreement the track was realigned and the curve eliminated. *Top* On 31 December 1960, an unidentified Standard '9F' 2-10-0 comes in off the ex-M&GN route from the East Coast, which lost its passenger service in February 1959. Note Stanier '8F' 2-8-0 No 48361 which had run through the trap points on the down goods loop and derailed itself. *H.N. James*

Middle Saxby is a junction no more as can be seen from this view recorded on 31 May 1988. The 11.05 Norwich to Birmingham New Street rushes past formed by 'Sprinters' Nos 156411 and 156402.

Above The old Saxby Junction looking west in 1956. The station, which closed on 6 February 1961, was situated just on the other side of the bridge in the background. Stanier '8F' 2-8-0 No 48386 makes a fine sight passing an unidentified classmate and battling against the elements on an eastbound freight. *H.N. James*

BOTTESFORD on the Great Northern Railway's Nottingham to Grantham line opened on 15 July 1850 and is the most northerly station in the county. 'K3' Class 2-6-0 No 61810 approaches the station on a Grantham-bound freight in September 1961. Note the lower quadrant signal. The 'K3' was withdrawn from Peterborough New England on 21 August 1962. *John F. Clay*

Bottesford station is still open today and is served by 17 trains each way on each weekday. On 31 August 1989 the 07.19 Birmingham New Street to Skegness train, unusually composed of InterCity coaching stock, runs in powered by Class '20' Nos 20212+20151. The crossing-keeper's cottage remains together with the manually operated crossing gates.

Rutland

The county of Rutland is now swallowed up by Leicestershire, but many local people still feel that it is a separate county with a character all of its own. The stone houses are reminiscent of Northamptonshire and the large expanse of water known by its former county name as Rutland Water is now an important tourist attraction.

OAKHAM: The former county town is the setting for Standard '5MT' 4-6-0 No 73011 at the station on a Nottingham to St Pancras express in 1957. *Ken Hunt*

Passing Oakham on 9 April 1991 is Class '60' No 60020 *Great Whernside* on a Lackenby to Corby steel train. The signal box is now a Grade 2 listed building and was used as the real-life model for the Airfix '00' gauge plastic kit for railway modellers.

MANTON JUNCTION on Saturday 6 May 1961, with Manton tunnel in the background. Stanier '5MT' 4-6-0 No 44658, new to Kentish Town shed in May 1949, takes the Kettering line with a local. The line leading out to the right of the picture is to Stamford and Peterborough and is the route used by the Birmingham to East Anglia 'Sprinter' trains. The Kettering line went over to freight-only in June 1966, the station at Manton closing the same month. This photograph was taken from the station footbridge which now no longer exists. *J.N. Faulkner*

The embankment alongside the Kettering line is as close to the position of the 1961 picture as is possible today. The date is 21 May 1989, and Class '58' No 58050 *Toton Diesel Depot* is on the 15.20 Leicester to St Pancras during the special InterCity 'Diesel Day' workings.

LUFFENHAM station in the 1950s with LNWR Webb 1890-design '1P' 2-4-2T No 46604 on the push-and-pull to Seaton. This elderly engine was the last but one to be withdrawn, going in September 1955 from Warwick shed. The station and line to Seaton closed on 6 June 1966. *John F. Clay*

By 10 July 1990 the station buildings had been demolished and only two tracks remain. The yard is now used by a haulage contractor. The 10.25 Birmingham to Norwich passes by, composed of 'Sprinter' set No 156427.

SEATON JUNCTION (1): Seaton was the junction for the double track line to Peterborough and the single track to Luffenham, all ex-LNWR territory. This was also the starting point for the branch to Uppingham. The Seaton to Stamford via Luffenham service was a push-and-pull working and had the distinction of being the last steam-operated train of this type in the country. The last performers were Ivatt 2-6-2T Nos 41212 and 41219, then a diesel multiple unit took over from 4 October 1965 until the lines in the area closed. This scene in 1964 has No 41212 in the bay platform with a Metro-Cammell DMU on the through line. *Hugh Ballantyne*

On 12 September 1989 this once busy station, set in rolling Rutland countryside, is now a memory. A scrapyard now occupies the site — and they call this progress!

SEATON JUNCTION (2): The station had its own one-road engine shed. Of wooden construction, it stood to the north of the station in the fork of the Peterborough and Luffenham lines. Built in 1894, it housed the engine used on the Uppingham branch, and was a sub-shed of Rugby, later changing its allegiance to Leicester Midland. On 29 April 1957 the shed was damaged by fire, but continued in use until closure in January 1961. This view of the shed, in August 1959, shows the fire-damaged building and Ivatt 2-6-2T No 41214 being prepared for work. This engine was built at Crewe and entered traffic in September 1948 at Crewe North shed. It was withdrawn in July 1965 from Templecombe shed on the S&D. *P.H. Groom*

The scrapyard has also taken over the shed building site. This photograph was also obtained on 12 September 1989.

SEATON JUNCTION (3): Just north of Seaton station was where the branch line to Uppingham and the line to Luffenham parted company. Running into Seaton off the Uppingham line on Saturday 28 May 1960 is Ivatt 2-6-2T No 41321. The 3³/₄-mile branch to Uppingham opened in September 1894 and was intended to serve the town's famous school, that institution being contracted with the LNWR to use the line. There was some goods traffic, but this never developed to any great extent. The ordinary passenger traffic was withdrawn on 13 June 1960, while school specials and goods trains ran for the last time on 30 May 1964. *Barry O. Hilton*

On 12 September 1989 little remains to suggest that the two railway lines actually ran, but the brick pw hut is still just visible.

UPPINGHAM station, the terminus of the branch. This is a September 1959 view and ex-LT&S '3P' 4-4-2T No 41975 quietly sees out its last days and awaits passengers on a mixed train back to Seaton Junction. This engine only lasted until December of that year, its last allocation being at Peterborough Spital Bridge depot. *P.H. Groom*

An engineering works producing hydraulic components now stands where the quiet country town station served the community. 12 September 1989.

NORTHAMPTONSHIRE

We start our tour of Northamptonshire in the county town itself. The main London & Birmingham line bypassed Northampton and took the route through Kilsby. It is said that this was because Northampton opposed the railway, but from past records it is apparent that the real reason was because the line's engineers, the Stephensons, favoured the more easily graded line missing Northampton. The town was, however, connected to the rail network in May 1845 when the London & Birmingham Railway opened the line from Blisworth, south of Northampton on the main London line, through to Peterborough. This linked the town to London Euston. It was not until 1882 that the route from Rugby through Northampton to Roade was opened and Castle station became the 'main line' station.

Northampton

NORTHAMPTON CASTLE (1): The station took its name from the nearby castle ruins which disappeared under the site of the goods shed built in 1880. This photograph, dated Tuesday 19 May 1964, has Willesden-based 'Britannia' 4-6-2 No 70014 *Iron Duke* approaching the north end of the station past No 2 signal box on a southbound coal train. Note the clips on the smoke deflector windshields which were once used for the 'Golden Arrow' decorations when the locomotive was the pride of Stewarts Lane shed in the 1950s. *L. Hanson*

On Thursday 11 May 1989 Class '87' electric locomotive No 87010 *King Arthur* passes the same spot on a diverted 13.30 Manchester to Euston express. This was unusual on a weekday and was probably due to a failure on the direct Kilsby route. The point of reference between the two photographs is the brick building on the right.

NORTHAMPTON CASTLE (2): Passing through on Saturday 17 June 1961 is Stanier '8F' 2-8-0 No 48657, a Rugby-based engine, on an up freight. This was one of the class built at Eastleigh Works in November 1943 and first allocated to Willesden. Withdrawal came in October 1964 from Bletchley shed. *Michael Mensing*

Castle station was rebuilt in 1965 as part of the electrification programme. The current was switched on for the first time from Hillmorton (Rugby) to Northampton on 6 June 1965 for insulation tests, and was later extended to Queens Park, London. Electrically-hauled freight trains ran as far as Northampton from the north from 26 July, and steam locomotives were finally withdrawn from the area on 27 September. The first recorded electrically-hauled passenger train appeared on 29 September when Class '85' No E3087 (85032) ran through as far as Bletchley on the 08.39 Carlisle to Euston due to the failure of the rostered diesel at Rugby. Twenty-three years later, on 8 June 1988, Class '81' No 81005, old number E3006, passes on the up 6E42 12.34 Liverpool Garston to Dagenham service conveying Ford cars from Halewood. No 81005 was withdrawn in February 1989.

NORTHAMPTON CASTLE (3): March-based Standard '4MT' 2-6-0 No 76032 stands in the No 5 bay platform on 17 June 1961, waiting to leave on the 17.10 to Peterborough East. Built at Doncaster in December 1953, its first allocation was to Stratford shed in London. Withdrawal came in August 1964 from Guildford shed — a very short life which hardly makes economic sense. *Michael Mensing*

By 8 June 1988 the station buildings and platforms have gone and in their place is the station car park. A link with the past is the metal girder bridge and the remains of the trackbed.

Lines south from Northampton

DUSTON WEST, on the line out to Blisworth, on Saturday 22 September 1951. The day before, 'Pacific' No 46207 *Princess Arthur of Connaught* had derailed itself at Heyford, near Weedon, on the 08.20 Liverpool to Euston express and this necessitated the diversion of all traffic through Northampton until the line was reopened on the 22nd. This view shows Carlisle Upperby-based rebuilt 'Royal Scot' 4-6-0 No 46146 *The Rifle Brigade* heading south to Euston on a diverted express from its home city. Crossing the bridge in the background on the line from Roade and about to enter Castle station is Stanier 4-6-0 No 45395. *L. Hanson*

What remains of the Blisworth line is hidden behind the bushes to the left of this June 1990 photograph. It is still used as a test track for the Chief Civil Engineer from the Bridge Street depot and terminates at buffer stops just outside Northampton town boundary, having closed to passenger traffic on 4 January 1960. It was, however, used until 3 January 1966 for diversions in connection with the electrification work on the main line. In the background a Class '90' electric locomotive heads a diverted down express into Northampton.

NORTHAMPTON BRIDGE STREET level crossing as Stanier 4-6-0 No 45139 (allocated to 14E, Bedford) runs over on the RCTS 'Grafton Rail Tour' on Sunday 9 August 1959. This tour had started from King's Cross and ran to Hitchin with Class '21' No D6101 in charge. '3F' 0-6-0 No 43474 then took over for the run to Bedford. Power from Bedford to Blisworth was No 45139, and for the next stage sister engine No 45091 took over to Woodford Halse and Banbury. On to Leamington ex-GWR 0-6-0PT No 3646 was employed, then ex-LMS power again in the shape of 4-6-0 No 44833 for the return via Braunston, Weedon, Leighton Buzzard, Dunstable and Luton. No D6101 took over again here and returned the seven-coach special (including essential refreshment car!) to King's Cross. If only it could still be repeated today. . . *L. Hanson*

On 10 July 1990 the signal box remains but the level crossing is now controlled by automatic barriers, and the footbridge has gone. The former Co-operative abattoir and pork factory over to the right is still with the same owners, but is now rebuilt as a superstore.

ROADE CUTTING: The ex-LNWR line south to Roade is the setting for this photograph of Standard 4-6-0 No 75038 on a Euston to Northampton local on Friday 10 August 1962. In the distance beyond the cutting the line passes through Roade station alongside the main line from Rugby in the upper right of the picture. The first mast for the coming electrification stands close to the overbridge. No 75038 had been built at Swindon and entered traffic at Bletchley in August 1953; it only lasted until November 1965, the last allocation being Shrewsbury. *L. Hanson*

On 28 July 1989 Class '86' electric No 86207 *City of Lichfield* has charge of the 17.15 Euston to Northampton. These trains, composed of Mk 1 carriage stock, earned the title 'Cobblers' and ran for the last time on Friday 11 May 1990, being replaced by Class '321' EMUs. The only marked difference between this and the 1962 scene is the intrusion of the overhead catenary, and the background chimney and mast.

ROADE station, looking north, on Saturday 17 March 1962. Stanier '5MT' 4-6-0 No 45237 runs in on an up parcels on the main line from Rugby. The station closed on 7 September 1964, and No 45237 'died' in September 1965 at Mold Junction. *Gerald Morgan*

On 10 July 1990 the station no longer exists, but the road bridge is our point of reference. Class '90' electric No 90010 *275 Railway Squadron (Volunteers)* speeds south on the 13.18 Holyhead to Euston.

TOWCESTER station on the ex-Stratford-upon-Avon & Midland Junction Railway. The line opened in May 1866 from Blisworth to Towcester and on to Cockley Brake and Banbury on 1 June 1872, the line to Stratford opening on 1 July 1873. In spite of Towcester being the junction for lines from Olney, Blisworth, Banbury and Stratford, it never developed as expected. The nearby racecourse, however, did attract specials, particularly on Easter Mondays when the Grafton Hunt steeplechases were staged. Even these specials succumbed in 1939, not to return after the war. The station closed on 5 April 1952 but the line remained open for freight until 1965. This view on 2 April 1960 shows LMS '4F' 0-6-0 No 44524 on a freight from Northampton. *Barry O. Hilton*

On 28 July 1989 a new industrial unit for a steel fabrication company has been built on the trackbed.

BYFIELD on the Towcester to Fenny Compton section of the S&MJ line. This was an SLS special, hauled by Bescot-based ex-LMS '4F' 0-6-0 No 44188, and was the last train over the line. The date is Saturday 24 April 1965, and this is the outward train from Birmingham Snow Hill via Stratford to Woodford Halse. The line from Woodford to Fenny Compton and Stratford was closed at short notice on 1 March, although the signal boxes at Kineton and Clifford Sidings remained staffed up to 15 March with no trains to signal, a situation which drew comment both locally and nationally, and even appeared on television! *Gerald Morgan*

An overall view of the former site of Byfield on 21 June 1991, now totally returned to nature.

Great Central through Northamptonshire

CATESBY TUNNEL: We return to the Great Central just south of Catesby tunnel near Charwelton on Saturday 19 September 1964. 'Royal Scot' Class 4-6-0 No 46156 *The South Wales Borderer* completes the climb and runs south on the 11.15 Nottingham Victoria to Marylebone parcels. No 46156 had not long to run, for it was withdrawn during the week ending 10 October 1964 from Annesley. *Hugh Ballantyne*

In June 1990 the trackbed is still clear of vegetation and in the background can be seen one of the smoke ventilation towers of Catesby tunnel.

CHARWELTON station, also on 19 September 1964. Standard '9F' 2-10-0 No 92014 heads north on a Woodford Halse to Annesley empty coal wagon train. The line running off to the right connected with the nearby ironstone quarries. The station had closed on 4 March 1963. *Hugh Ballantyne*

The June 1990 comparison shot had to be made slightly to the left of the 1964 photograph as the view is now obscured by the tree on the right. The station and road overbridge have disappeared entirely.

WOODFORD HALSE: The nameboard at the station once proclaimed 'Junction for the Great Western Railway, Dover, Folkestone and Stratford-upon-Avon'. Before the railway arrived, Woodford was a quiet village but developed with the new job opportunities that came with the railway age. A locomotive depot was provided along with extensive yards controlled by four signal boxes. An unidentified Stanier '5MT' 4-6-0 leaves Woodford Halse on a two-coach local to Banbury on Saturday 18 August 1962. The line connecting the GC to the GWR at Banbury (middle distance, left) opened on 1 June 1900. Woodford closed completely with the abandonment of the Great Central from Rugby to Aylesbury on 3 September 1966. Local trains had been withdrawn from 4 March 1963 and Woodford shed closed on 14 June 1965. The last allocation was 17 engines, all ex-LMS types: 42082/44762/44764/44814/48002/48005/48010/48011/48035/48061/48081/48088/48121/48336/48506/48517/48527. *R.K. Kirkland*

June 1990 and the same view from the bridge that once spanned the track. The only movement now is from the occupants of the pig farm seen in their enclosures. 'Pigs' used to run past here occasionally in steam days, for this was the nickname given to the Ivatt '4MT' 2-6-0s that appeared from time to time.

WOODFORD WEST JUNCTION, the other end of the spur from the Great Central to the SMJ. The crew of '2251' Class 0-6-0 No 2246 check with the signalman on their path down to Woodford station in readiness to join '43XX' 2-6-0 No 6368 for the 12 October 1963 LCGB 'Thames-Avon and Severn' railtour. *Gerald Morgan*

A junction no more — the trackbed is now owned by a local farmer. Surprisingly, the footbridge in the background still survives.

BRACKLEY CENTRAL: *Top* An excellent view of the station on 18 July 1959, showing the distinctive railway architecture and island platform. Ex-LNER 'V2' Class 2-6-2 No 60879 returns home north with the 12.15 Marylebone to Manchester. *J.N. Faulkner*

Middle Brackley station buildings are now an ATS tyre-fitting centre and a great deal of the trackbed has been infilled. Note the 1953 AEC Regal Mark 4 coach, ex-BEA-owned, standing where the up main line used to be.

Above A further view of the station on 18 July 1959 looking south. Neasden-based Standard '4MT' 2-6-4T No 80140 arrives with the 12.32 from Marylebone. No 80140 outlasted the Central, being withdrawn on 9 July 1967 from London Nine Elms depot. *J.N. Faulkner*

BRACKLEY (LNW): The town boasted two stations and this is the ex-LNWR one photographed on Saturday 6 August 1960. The line ran from Banbury Merton Street through Buckingham to join the Bletchley to Oxford line at Verney Junction. The Bletchley to Banbury section opened on 1 May 1850 and the Verney Junction to Oxford on 20 May 1851. The Banbury line remained as a branch line throughout. In 1956 British Railways selected the route as an experiment in the use of single railcars in an attempt to save costs, and with them rural branch lines that were making a loss. Two single-car Derby Lightweight units were built and numbered M79900 and M79901, and they here form the 15.45 Banbury to Buckingham calling at Brackley. However, despite cutting the deficit quite substantially, the branch did not survive and closed on 2 January 1961. Unit M79900 has survived in departmental stock at Derby Railway Technical Centre as RDB975010 and is currently the subject of a possible preservation appeal. *Michael Mensing*

The former station site was particularly difficult to find as there is now no evidence of a railway at all — even the stone bridge has disappeared. Immediately behind the photographer is a newly-built police station; indeed, this 1990 photograph was obtained by standing in its doorway.

Lines north of Northampton

KILSBY TUNNEL: We return to the ex-LNWR 'Premier Line' at Kilsby tunnel. Had Stephenson known the trouble he would encounter when boring through the uplands at this location, he may have had second thoughts about taking this route. Some idea of the likely strata to be found was already known, as 30 years before the results of investigations into building a tunnel for the nearby Grand Union canal were available; quicksand had been found which decided the canal engineers to build further eastwards. The trial borings for the railway tunnel, however, did not indicate this problem. Contractor James Nowell commenced work in 1834 and very soon after quicksand was encountered and the workings flooded. So sudden was the incursion that the workmen had to swim for their lives. Powerful pumping equipment was brought in capable of removing 2,000 gallons of water per minute, but even so operations were held up for eight months. The contractor then became bankrupt and the railway company, the London & Birmingham, had to take over the work. Only after an outlay of £300,000 and a very great cost in human life was the tunnel completed, with the last brick being placed in the lining on 21 June 1838. There are nine ventilation shafts surmounted by stone towers and over three million bricks were used in the construction. Passing the board announcing the tunnel's length on Saturday 23 August 1958 is 'Jubilee' Class 4-6-0 No 45688 *Polyphemus* on an up extra. *Barry O. Hilton*

On 28 July 1989 Class '85' electric No 85025 emerges from Kilsby tunnel on the 15.25 Wolverhampton to Euston. Since this photograph was taken, all West Midlands to Euston services are now rostered for Driving Van Trailers at the south end of the train with the locomotive pushing at the rear.

WEEDON station, between Kilsby and Roade. Ex-LNWR '7F' 0-8-0 No 49094 plods south on a freight composed of chalk wagons on Saturday 18 January 1958; the station closed on 15 September the same year. No 49094 also featured earlier in this book at Countesthorpe (see page 32). *Michael Mensing*

Where Weedon station used to be on 10 July 1990, one week after a £700,000 track re-alignment to remove a speed restriction. Class '87' electric No 87032 *Kenilworth* passes by on the 14.33 Carlisle to Euston.

Rugby to Market Harborough line

LILBOURNE: On Saturday 24 April 1965 the 12.40 Harwich to Rugby, powered by Class '24' 1160 hp diesel No D5010, later to become No 24010, calls at Lilbourne, near the Warwickshire border. This locomotive was withdrawn in October 1975 and cut up in January 1977 at Doncaster Works. The line was closed on 6 June 1966. *Michael Mensing*

Hard to believe, but this is the same spot on 8 June 1988, with the remains of the level crossing gatepost and platform fence-post as the only railway clues. The M1 motorway can just be seen in the background on both past and present views.

YELVERTOFT AND STANFORD PARK station, the next one along the line towards Market Harborough, recorded on Saturday 2 October 1965. It is once again the 12.40 Harwich to Rugby passing by with Class '24' diesel No D5012 (later No 24012) in charge. This one was withdrawn in August 1975 and also cut up at Doncaster Works, in February 1976. *Michael Mensing*

Now a private clubhouse, Yelvertoft down-side station buildings still remain, complete with old-style telephone box. The date of this photograph is 8 June 1988.

Northampton to Market Harborough line

The 18-mile ex-LNWR branch from Northampton to Market Harborough opened on 16 February 1859. It was double track throughout and was steeply graded in parts, all up goods trains from Market Harborough requiring banking assistance to Kelmarsh in steam days. The line served the ironstone workings at Pitsford and Lamport and the stations along the route were situated where local roads crossed the line by level crossings, and many were over a mile from the villages they purported to serve. Closure to passenger traffic took place on 4 January 1960. The last train to Market Harborough left Northampton Castle station at 20.33 on 2 January with 2-6-2T No 41218 in charge. This engine should have returned on the last departure from Market Harborough but, no doubt overcome by the occasion, was declared a failure. It was left to 2-6-4T No 42331 to take out the last train, which arrived back at Northampton 58 minutes late at 22.59. In January 1969 the Midland sleeper services were diverted away from St Pancras and a single train was provided from Euston at 21.00 which ran over the line to gain the Midland at Market Harborough. Excursion traffic also ran over the route from time to time. Freight trains continued to use the line until final closure took place on 15 August 1981.

KELMARSH: This view of Northampton-based 2-6-4T No 42353 is at Kelmarsh on a Market Harborough train in 1959. *Chris Banks*
 On 11 May 1989 the station buildings have gone and nature has reclaimed its territory.

CLIPSTON AND OXENDON on 16 May 1959. Ivatt 2-6-2T No 41218 is on the 15.45 Northampton to Market Harborough. Note the less than standard height of the platforms with their attendant steps. *Barry O. Hilton*

On 11 May 1989 the trackbed is still recognisable and the old station house is a privately owned residence, now hidden from view behind the trees on the right.

Midland Main Line

DESBOROUGH AND ROTHWELL, between Market Harborough and Kettering, on Easter Monday, 22 April 1957. 'Jubilee' 4-6-0 No 45554 *Ontario* approaches the station from the south on the 12.50 St Pancras to Leicester. This section of line opened for passengers on 8 May 1857 as far as Bedford; Desborough and Rothwell station closed on 1 January 1968. *Michael Mensing*

On 10 July 1990 Class '56' No 56057 runs past the same spot on the 10.40 Brentford to Bardon Hill empties. It was not possible to stand in exactly the same position as the 1957 photograph as this is now occupied by a storage shed. The goods shed still stands and its yard is now used as a haulage depot, while behind the photographer the station house still survives as a private residence. Nature has taken over the embankment and hidden the railway fence, and the telegraph poles, for so long a Midland line feature, have also disappeared.

KETTERING (1): The north end of the station on Thursday 6 May 1954, as Compound 4-4-0 No 41075 runs in on the 16.23 Leicester to St Pancras. Built in 1924 at Derby, No 41075 lasted until April 1957, its last allocation being Bradford Manningham. On the right is the yard of the locomotive depot situated alongside the station on the up side. Dating back to around 1876, it was a brick-built four-road structure with coaling stage and turntable. On 1 January 1949 Kettering's allocation consisted of 35 locomotives, and a similar total remained until closure on 14 June 1965. *J.N. Faulkner*

The steam age railway equipment has disappeared by 21 May 1989, and the signals are now colour lights. The 17.38 Sundays-only Nottingham to St Pancras runs through headed by HST power car No 43048.

KETTERING (2): A view looking south from the end of the down main platform. The date is Wednesday 14 October 1964 and Kettering-based Stanier '8F' 2-8-0 No 48107 runs down the main on an iron ore train. Kettering Station signal box stands in the background and has since been preserved by the Midland Railway Trust at Swanwick. No 48107 lasted until April 1968, its last operating home being Heaton Mersey. *K.C.H. Fairey*

By 20 July 1989 the signal box and signals had gone, together with most of the sidings, all replaced by a more rationalised layout and modern signalling for today's high-speed workings (Kettering was manually signalled up until 1986). The 16.30 St Pancras to Nottingham runs in with HST power car No 43098 leading.

KETTERING (3): No 2 (up) platform on Monday 30 March 1959. Locally-shedded 2MT 2-6-0 No 46495 waits to leave on a three-coach local to Huntingdon (see page 99). Built under British Railways at Darlington in 1952, No 46495 went new to Kettering in January. Only enjoying a short life, withdrawal came in October 1966 from Crewe South. *K.C.H. Fairey*

Kettering station still retains its canopies and is virtually unchanged and well worth a visit. Class '108' DMU Nos 51571+59163+59734+53628 has arrived at platform 2 from Corby on 20 July 1989 and will return at 17.37. Sadly, the passenger service was withdrawn on 2 June 1990 as a direct result of Northamptonshire Council stopping its financial support. The station at Corby has been mothballed for possible future use, and a fight now seems inevitable to try and have the service restored.

FINEDON station, midway between Kettering and Wellingborough, on Thursday 3 May 1962. Standard '5MT' 4-6-0 No 73142 runs past on a down fitted goods back to its home base, Rowsley, as the lineside workers take a break. Finedon station building is in the background, and had closed to passengers as long ago as 2 December 1940. Caprotti valve gear-fitted No 73142 lasted until May 1968, being withdrawn from Manchester Patricroft. *K.C.H. Fairey*

On 16 June 1990 the station buildings, sidings, signal box and goods lines have all gone, but the road overbridge remains in the background as the point of reference. HST power car No 43100 runs nonchalantly past on the 12.30 St Pancras to Nottingham.

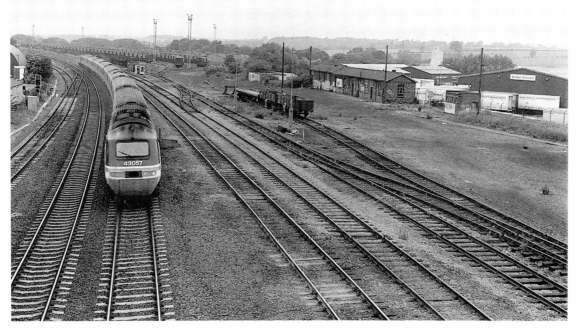

WELLINGBOROUGH FINEDON ROAD yard with home-based Crosti-boilered '9F' 2-10-0 No 92028 sorting out its train on Thursday 16 July 1959. A '4F' 0-6-0 waits behind to back down into the yard. The 2-10-0 is using its unconventional boiler in this photograph, hence the smoke being emitted from the side and not at the front. This locomotive was modified to a normally operating boiler on 3 December 1959, but retained the non-standard look without smoke deflectors until withdrawal from Saltley depot in October 1966. *K.C.H. Fairey*

On 16 June 1990 there are still sidings, but they are now much reduced in status and size, with redundant MGR wagons the usual occupants. HST power car No 43057 leads a Nottingham to St Pancras express.

WELLINGBOROUGH MIDLAND ROAD (1): The north end of the station on Sunday 15 June 1958. 'Jubilee' Class 4-6-0 No 45597 *Barbados*, **with a complete absence of any steam escaping, drifts through on the 16.15 St Pancras to Bradford express.** *K.C.H. Fairey*

On 7 November 1990, a possibly never-to-be-repeated scene — brand new Foster Yeoman-owned Class '59' No 59104 heads north through Wellingborough station on a test train back to Derby. Delivery to this country from America had taken place on Saturday 20 October and this was one of the trial runs back from Cricklewood, with speeds of up to 80 mph, to assess whether stone trains could run at 75 mph. The train was composed of five Mk 3 sleepers and a test coach.

WELLINGBOROUGH MIDLAND ROAD (2): Wellingborough occasionally played host to specials in steam days, and this is the scene on Sunday 7 March 1965. Maunsell 'U' Class 2-6-0 No 31639 pilots Bulleid 'Q1' Class 0-6-0 No 33006 on a Home Counties Railway Society 'Six Counties' special. This was a circular tour from Paddington and ran via Fenny Compton, Stratford-upon-Avon, Leamington Spa, Rugby, Northampton, Wellingborough London Road, round to Midland Road, and back via Oxford. Both locomotives were withdrawn in 1966, No 31639 from Guildford in June and No 33006 in January from the same depot. *Horace A. Gamble*

Twenty-four years later, on Sunday 21 May 1989, history repeats itself at Wellingborough with two Southern Region locomotives on a special — Class '33' diesels Nos 33021 (in Railfreight Construction livery) and 33022 on an InterCity 'Diesel Day' working from St Pancras to Leicester.

WELLINGBOROUGH MIDLAND ROAD (3): The south end of the station on Saturday 26 May 1956 is the setting for this rare photograph of the Higham Ferrers branch train (see page 98) being hauled by Belpaire-boilered ex-L&Y Aspinall '2P' 2-4-2T No 50650. This was not a type usually associated with this part of the world, but No 50650 had been transferred from Royston (20C) to Wellingborough during March 1956, to replace ex-Midland 0-4-4T No 58080 which had been withdrawn in January. A second example, No 50646, had also been sent further south to Bedford but, after two attempts at passenger work and failing each time, was confined to shed duties only. Wellingborough obviously got the better deal, and this engine made the first appearance of this class at Northampton on 2 April after working the 17.40 from Wellingborough. Its use, however, was short-lived, for it was withdrawn during the first week in October, so ending an interesting few months in Wellingborough shed's history. *K.C.H. Fairey*

Photographed from a little further over, next to the main line at the south end of Wellingborough station, on 20 July 1989, HST power car No 43053 *County of Humberside* heads the 14.37 Nottingham to St Pancras. Note that the wooden huts in the background have, remarkably, survived.

WELLINGBOROUGH MIDLAND ROAD (4): Our last look at the Midland Main Line, south of Wellingborough station. This view, from Irthlingborough Road bridge, has an up Bradford to St Pancras express approaching in true LMS style with '2P' 4-4-0 No 40632 piloting 'Jubilee' 4-6-0 No 45649 *Hawkins*. The date is Tuesday 2 June 1959. Note St Mary's church in the background and the 'Morris Motors' water tower on the right; the latter was the site of Thomas Butlin's iron ore smelting furnaces opened in 1867. They closed in 1926 and were dismantled in 1930. The Morris Motors plant was built on the site in 1947-50. *K.C.H. Fairey*

Thirty years later, on 21 May 1989, Class '47' No 47347, in Railfreight Metal sector livery, passes the same spot on the 16.48 Leicester to St Pancras special. The water tower still stands, but now with the old British Leyland company logo.

WELLINGBOROUGH LONDON ROAD (1): We remain in Wellingborough and move to the ex-LNWR station at London Road, on the line from Northampton Bridge Street to Wansford and Peterborough East. The spur line between the two Wellingborough stations (see opposite) was opened in 1857 by the Midland and carried passenger traffic from 1 October 1866; the Midland also shared running powers with the LNWR through to Northampton. By 1961 the service was nine push-and-pull trains each way plus a through train to Nottingham, returning from Leicester. Closure took effect from 4 May 1964, together with the Peterborough section. This photograph was recorded on 2 May, the last Saturday of operation. Ivatt 2-6-2T No 41225 heads the 12.25 Northampton to Wellingborough Midland Road push-and-pull working. *J.N. Faulkner*

On 20 July 1989 Wellingborough London Road is just a memory. Behind the photographer, the new A45 road crosses the trackbed. The only point of reference in this photograph is the Whitworth's silos at the top left-hand corner.

Below A second look at the station showing the up-side station buildings and yard in more detail. Willesden 'Black Five' No 45324 (unusually clean for an engine from this depot) draws to a halt at London Road with the 16.54 to Northampton on Saturday 28 May 1960. August 1967 was the withdrawal month for No 45324, last allocation **Heaton Mersey.** *K.C.H. Fairey*

WELLINGBOROUGH LONDON ROAD (2): Crossing over the River Nene on the spur from Wellingborough London Road to Midland Road is Beyer-Garratt 2-6-6-2T No 47969 on an iron ore train on Wednesday 26 June 1957. This mighty machine had not long to live, being withdrawn from Hasland during the week ending 3 August the same year. *K.C.H. Fairey*

The only photograph that Mrs Milner was allowed to take! The bridge is still in position on 20 July 1989 and walking along the old trackbed is Chris and daughter Sarah.

Higham Ferrers branch

It was originally intended to extend this $3^1/_2$-mile branch from Wellingborough through to Raunds to link with the Kettering to Huntingdon line, but a local landowner refused to sell his land so the line was only built to this old market town. Goods traffic commenced on 1 September 1893, and passenger services on 1 May 1894, running until 15 June 1959. However, through trains to Blackpool and Yarmouth and return continued to run until 1964, but only on Saturdays during the August holiday fortnight. The return Blackpool trains were steam-worked to the end and were rostered for a Blackpool engine, usually a Stanier '5MT'. Freight continued up the line until November 1969.

HIGHAM FERRERS on Saturday 25 August 1962, with Willesden's Fowler 2-6-4T No 42350 on the RCTS 'Fernie' railtour. The engine had been sent up to Northampton shed a few days before and specially cleaned. The tour had started at Northampton and included Market Harborough, Uppingham, Wansford, Peterborough, Manton, Oakham and Higham Ferrers in its itinerary. The station building still remained at this date and it was discovered that a stock of printed tickets to other local stations was still held, some being sold to the tour patrons as souvenirs!
Photomatic

On 16 June 1990 even the road overbridge has been removed. The photographer's car is the only 'motive power' present.

Kettering to Huntingdon branch

This line opened to goods traffic on 21 February 1866 and to passengers one week later as the Kettering, Thrapstone & Huntingdon Railway. The Midland worked the line from the beginning (although it did not become vested in the Midland until 6 August 1897) and had running rights over Great Eastern metals onward to Cambridge. As with the Higham Ferrers branch, passenger services ceased on 15 June 1959 and freight from 4 July 1969.

BARTON SEAGRAVE, a few miles out from Kettering, on Thursday 28 May 1959. Ivatt '2MT' 2-6-0 No 46403 (new to Derby during the week ending 14 December 1946 and transferred to Kettering during the week ending 21 June 1947) works the 14.10 to Cambridge. *K.C.H. Fairey*

On 16 June 1990 the right-hand embankment is still just recognisable, but the left-hand side of the trackbed is being excavated for the new A1/M1 link road (A14).

Seaton to Wansford and Peterborough

WAKERLEY AND BARROWDEN: The ex-LNWR line to Peterborough from Seaton via Wansford is the setting for this view at Wakerley and Barrowden, not far from Seaton. Class 'J39' 0-6-0 No 64891 passes on an eastbound freight in 1955. The engine was allocated to Peterborough Spital Bridge depot at the time, and was withdrawn on 8 February 1960 from March. Closure for the line was 6 June 1966. *John F. Clay*

On 12 September 1989 little evidence remains of a railway other than part of the station building on the left of the photograph.

WANSFORD station on 25 August 1962, and another look at the RCTS 'Fernie' railtour with Fowler 2-6-4T No 42350 in charge. *R.H.G. Simpson*

Wansford is now preserved as part of the Nene Valley Railway. After a successful enthusiasts' day, former BR Class '14' diesel-hydraulics Nos D9523 and D9516 head an engineers train on 15 September 1990. Built at Swindon Works in 1964, both locomotives were withdrawn on 1 April 1968 and sold to the British Steel Corporation for use at their quarries in Northamptonshire. *Michael J. Collins*

CAMBRIDGESHIRE

The Soke of Peterborough was at one time a separate county, but is now swallowed up into Cambridgeshire. The first railway to reach the city was opened on 2 June 1845; this was the London & Birmingham branch from Blisworth and Northampton and terminated at the Eastern Counties Railway premises, later to be known as Peterborough East. The next arrival to share this station was the Midland Railway from Stamford, opening on 2 October 1846. The ECR's line from Ely was not completed for goods traffic until December 1846, being opened to passengers on 14 January 1847.

Peterborough

PETERBOROUGH EAST (1): On Whit Monday, 6 June 1960, the 12.40 to Northampton via Wellingborough, over the Nene Valley line, is powered by Fowler 2-6-4T No 42353. *Michael Mensing*

By Saturday 10 September 1988 Peterborough East station has been swept away, although evidence of the platform can just be seen, and a few sidings remain. The site of the goods shed on the left was being prepared for a car park. The picture is completed by Class '47' No 47143 with a rake of Network SouthEast stock on the 13.40 Yarmouth to Birmingham New Street.

102

PETERBOROUGH EAST (2): Looking in the opposite direction from the previous photograph, Class '4F' 0-6-0 No 44034 approaches Peterborough East on the 07.28 Birmingham New Street to Peterborough on 6 June 1960. Crossing the girder bridges in the background is the Great Northern main line from King's Cross, and the line leading off to the left is the Nene Valley route to Wansford and Northampton. No 44034 was withdrawn in June 1963 from Leicester Midland depot. *Michael Mensing*

Class '47' No 47143 again, on the outward run from Birmingham to Yarmouth on 10 September 1988, timed to leave New Street at 07.50. Significant differences are the additional pylon, seen lying on its side awaiting erection in the 1960 photograph, and the absence of semaphore signals. Also, the first line into Peterborough, the Nene Valley, has been removed.

PETERBOROUGH NORTH (1): We now move to the main-line station (see also page 4), full of character and steam age atmosphere. The date is 6 June 1960 and '3P2F' 'N2/2' 0-6-2T No 69521 plays around with some parcels vans in the south-end bay platform. This was once a King's Cross-based engine and still has the condensing apparatus used when working through the Metropolitan 'Widened Lines' tunnels. By this date it had been sent north to work out its last days, withdrawal coming on 1 June 1961. *Michael Mensing*

Photographed from the same position, the road bridge spanning the tracks at the south end, on 10 September 1988, HST power car No 43096 heads the 07.35 Newcastle to King's Cross out of the completely remodelled station.

PETERBOROUGH NORTH (2): Looking back towards the station from Spital Bridge, which spans the lines just to the north. Note Peterborough Cathedral, over a mile from the station, on the skyline to the left. Making its way over to the ex-Midland tracks is the 17.32 Peterborough East to Leicester, hauled by '4F' 0-6-0 No 44521 on 6 June 1960. The ex-Midland roundhouse was situated just off the picture to the right; this closed on 1 February 1960 and was demolished soon afterwards. In the 1930s Peterborough had four operating locomotive depots, the ex-Great Northern at New England (with workshops), the ex-Great Eastern and LNWR near Peterborough East and, as already mentioned, the ex-Midland Spital Bridge depot. By June 1960 only New England remained. *Michael Mensing*

Twenty-nine years later, on 25 June 1989, Class '91' electric locomotive No 91007 leaves with the Sundays-only 16.40 King's Cross to Leeds.

PETERBOROUGH NORTH (3): The view looking north from Spital Bridge. Over on the left are the ex-Midland tracks to Stamford and Melton. Running on the main line is 'V2' Class 2-6-2 No 60930 on an up relief at 17.29 on 6 June 1960. Looking here in excellent condition, No 60930 only lasted until 1962, for withdrawal from Doncaster shed came on 23 September. In the far distance beyond the multi-arch bridge are New England yards and on the horizon can just be seen the coaling tower for the motive power depot, which was home for over 100 steam locomotives at this time. *Michael Mensing*

On 10 September 1988 Class '156' 'Sprinter' No 156422 comes off the up goods loop after allowing an HST to pass. The train is the 11.35 Liverpool Lime Street to Norwich, one of the high-mileage runs these units now operate daily.

Cambridge

The railway arrived at Cambridge in 1845 when the Eastern Counties Railway opened its route through to Norwich from London. The station, situated a mile from the town centre, opened on 30 July. Its main single platform, with a scissor crossing at the centre, remains today with bay platforms at each end.

CAMBRIDGE (1): This 1950s view shows elderly 'J15' 0-6-0 No 65456 standing alongside the main platform on empty coaching stock. No 65456 was withdrawn from stock on 8 September 1958, last allocation Colchester, and was scrapped at Stratford Works. *G.W. Sharpe*

Alongside the platform on 4 August 1989 is Class '47' No 47581 *Great Eastern* in charge of the 17.08 Cambridge to Liverpool Street. Following on from the electrification programme, these services are now entrusted to electric multiple units and this locomotive was transferred over to the Western Region at Old Oak Common.

CAMBRIDGE (2): Stanier 2-6-4T No 42666 has the signal for its Cambridge to Bletchley train, standing here in the south bay platform. This 1950s scene shows all the trappings of the steam age railway, now disappeared. No 42666 finally succumbed to modernisation during the week ending 29 September 1962, its last home being Barrow-in-Furness. *H.N. James*

The modern scene at Cambridge, recorded on 4 August 1989, and stabled in the bay platform is EMU No 317342. Also further to the left are Cravens diesel departmental units TDB977123 and TDB977125. Dominating the background in this and the earlier view is the grain warehouse which is still in use.

CAMBRIDGE (3): The north end of the station, and Class 'B17/6' 'Sandringham' Class 4-6-0 No 61636 *Harlaxton Manor* pilots BR Standard 'Britannia' 4-6-2 No 70039 *Sir Christopher Wren* on the Sunday 08.24 Liverpool Street to Norwich via Cambridge, passing the North signal box on 27 April 1958. No 61636 was withdrawn from Norwich on 21 October 1959 and No 70039 ended its career at Carlisle Kingmoor during the week ending 23 September 1967. *Brian Morrison*

Far less interesting is the departure of EMU No 310069, empty stock to Coldham Lane carriage sidings, on 10 May 1989. Gone is the North signal box and along with it the manual signalling, replaced by the all-pervading modern colour lights.

Lines south of Cambridge

TRUMPINGTON: The Great Eastern main line south from Cambridge at Trumpington, about 2 miles out from the city, showing the extensive yards that once existed here. This was the junction for the LNWR line through Sandy and Bedford to Bletchley. Class 'E4' 2-4-0 No 62784 runs past with a Sudbury and Marks Tey train in 1953. This design dated back to 1891 and No 62784 was withdrawn on 30 May 1955 from Cambridge shed. *H.N. James*

On 10 May 1989 the railway is now reduced to just two tracks. Electric multiple unit No 321329 runs past with the 12.02 from Cambridge to Liverpool Street.

SHEPRETH BRANCH JUNCTION: This was the dividing point for the Great Eastern main line to Liverpool Street and the Great Northern branch to King's Cross via Hitchin. The latter line had been completed in April 1852, but it was not until 1866 that through services operated from King's Cross to Cambridge. The intervening years had seen the line leased by the Eastern Counties Railway with only a sparse service from Hitchin. This 1950s view shows 'WD' 'Austerity' 2-8-0 No 90023 of March (31B) shed taking the main line towards Shelford with a southbound empties. This Riddles-designed engine was withdrawn from Tilbury shed on 7 September 1962. *H.N. James*

Now part of the electrified system, the location is still a junction performing the same important role, but now overseen by power signalling, the old manually operated box gone for ever. On 10 May 1989 EMU No 321338 takes the Liverpool Street route on the 11.02 from Cambridge.

SHELFORD: Just south of Shepreth Branch Junction on the main line to Liverpool Street is Shelford station with its level crossing. This 1961 view, taken from the end of the up platform, sees 'B1' Class 4-6-0 No 61236 running through on a mixed freight for Cambridge. This locomotive entered traffic in September 1947 and was first allocated to London's Stratford depot. It finished its days at March, withdrawal coming on 16 September 1962. *H.N. James*

Shelford station is still open and is served on weekdays by around 20 trains each way. On 4 August 1989 Class '31' No 31144 passes with a Duxford to March Speedlink working. The crossing is now controlled by automatic barriers instead of the signal box, but 'The Railway Tavern' is still there in the background, although now without its chimneys.

Bartlow branch

In 1865 the Eastern Counties Railway opened a branch from Shelford through Bartlow to Sudbury. Known as the Stour Valley line, it was single track with passing places at the stations along its route. Railbuses were introduced from 7 July 1958, but the line did not prove profitable and closed completely on 6 March 1967.

LINTON station, between Shelford and Bartlow, on 23 July 1966. Class '31' No D5656 runs in with the single line token on the Summer Saturdays 14.00 Clacton to Leicester London Road. A first-generation diesel multiple unit waits for the road on the 15.30 Cambridge to Sudbury. *G.R. Mortimer*

To obtain an identical view on 10 May 1989 it was necessary to photograph from the second floor of an engineering factory which is now built across the path of the track. The station now forms the offices for the company, Walden Precision Apparatus Ltd, and the original stationmaster's house alongside is a private residence.

BARTLOW: The next station along the line was Bartlow, which was the junction for the branch to Audley End via Saffron Walden. This line opened on 22 October 1866 and closed on 7 September 1964. In this view, recorded at Bartlow on 27 April 1958, the Audley End line runs in from the left. Ivatt '2MT' 2-6-0 No 46467 heads the 14.02 local from Cambridge to Marks Tey. No 46467 was built at Darlington Works and entered traffic on 29 June 1951 at Cambridge. Withdrawal came on 23 July 1964 from Dumfries. Bartlow was the scene for a sequence in the film *The Virgin Soldiers* filmed in September 1968. Withdrawn Stanier 'Black Five' No 44781 was towed to Bartlow and lowered into a specially dug pit, having been supposedly blown up by guerrillas in the Malayan jungle. *Brian Morrison*

On 10 May 1989, a surprising survivor is the derelict signal box now alongside a farm track which occupies the old trackbed. Behind the photographer the original station building still stands, now transformed into a substantial private house surrounded by rolling lawns. The retaining wall is also still intact to the right of the photograph.

CAMPS CUTTING, east of Bartlow, was the longest and deepest on any single-line railway in England; from rail level to the top of the bridge was 50 feet. 'E4' Class 2-4-0 No 62785 provides a 'Driver Training' run for members of the Cambridge University Railway Club on Sunday 27 April 1958. This was an annual event for the railway-minded undergraduates to try their hand at steam locomotive driving and firing, under supervision of Cambridge shed staff, and they had this part of the line to themselves. No 62785 dated back to 1891 and was withdrawn from Cambridge on 7 December 1959. It was the last of the class to remain active. *Brian Morrison*

Camps Cutting is now no more, for the whole length was filled in with builders' waste material. Filling-in commenced in 1974 and was not completed until 1987. All that remains in this May 1989 view is the top level of bricks which formed the parapet of the bridge in the 1958 photograph.

St Neots

ST NEOTS: We return to the East Coast Main Line briefly on 20 July 1961 at St Neots. Standard '9F' 2-10-0 No 92184 runs through on an up Presflo wagon train. Note the impressive signals. *Author's Collection*

St Neots station is now modernised and part of the Network SouthEast operation with a busy commuter customer base. The 14.10 Leeds to King's Cross speeds through on 22 May 1991 with DVT No 82209 leading and Class '91' No 91016 providing the power at the rear.

St Ives to Cambridge branch

The line from Chesterton Junction, Cambridge, to St Ives opened on 17 August 1847 and onwards to March on 1 February 1848. It eventually became part of the Great Eastern Railway and was an early candidate for dieselisation, multiple units being introduced from 3 November 1958. However, steam passenger trains could still be seen up to 15 June 1959, for this was the route taken by the Kettering to Cambridge services. The last passenger train ran on Saturday 3 October 1970, leaving St Ives at 22.00 and calling at all stations instead of running to Cambridge non-stop as on normal Saturdays. This followed the unsuccessful campaign by St Ives borough councillors to keep the line open. Part of the line from Cambridge to Fen Drayton is still open for sand traffic from the extensive workings in the area.

ST IVES JUNCTION station on 2 October 1970. At the far end of the station is Class '31' No 5532 on a Cambridge freight, recorded again overleaf at Long Stanton. A Park Royal DMU also awaits departure for Cambridge. The trackbed to the left is the lifted line to Huntingdon which closed in the 1960s. *G.R. Mortimer*

The rail-less scene on 22 May 1991 had to be taken from ground level as the station footbridge, which was the vantage point for the 1970 view, is long gone. Most of the station buildings have been demolished, but a small part remains in use as offices.

LONG STANTON: This photograph, also taken on 2 October 1970, again shows Class '31' No 5532 on the St Ives to Cambridge freight. *G.R. Mortimer*

On 10 May 1989 Class '31' Nos 31134 and 31128 head towards Cambridge along the now single track with the 08.30 Fen Drayton to King's Cross sand train. The station buildings still stand and are now used as offices.

HISTON station. The date is 19 September 1970 and a Cravens DMU arrives on a St Ives to Cambridge service, despite showing 'St Ives' on the destination blind. Note the unusual positioning, on the left of the photograph, of the home signal, to give a better view to Cambridge-bound drivers; just discernible is another photographer up the post. This photograph was also taken from a signal on the approach to Histon. *G.R. Mortimer*

The 08.30 Fen Drayton to King's Cross sand train is photographed for a second time on 10 May 1989 at Histon. Its progress along the branch is particularly slow as the level crossing gates have to be opened and closed by the train crew. This view had to be taken from ground level as the signal post had gone!

Ely to Newmarket line

ELY (1): The city had its first railway connection in 1845 when the line from London to Norwich opened on 30 July. Other routes to Kings Lynn and Peterborough opened in 1847 and to Newmarket in 1879. This view, on 4 May 1957, shows Cambridge-based 'D16/3' 4-4-0 No 62530 leaving on the 16.50 to Northampton. This 4-4-0 moved to March shed in October 1957 and was withdrawn from there on 22 September 1958. *J.N. Faulkner*

By 9 September 1989 the small shunting signal at the end of the platform has been replaced by an ordinary home signal which will also be removed during the re-signalling as part of the Cambridge to Kings Lynn electrification. 'Sprinter' No 156429 leaves on a Liverpool to Norwich service.

ELY (2): Looking northwards over the boarded level crossing on 4 May 1957. 'B12/3' 4-6-0 No 61516 runs in on the 14.25 Hunstanton to Liverpool Street. This locomotive had originally been built at Stratford Works in 1913 and was rebuilt in November 1932. Withdrawal came on 14 July 1958 from Cambridge shed. *J.N. Faulkner*

On 9 September 1989 Class '47' No 47579 *James Nightall G.C.* heads the 13.20 Kings Lynn to Cambridge over the now tarmac-covered crossing. The locomotive was named to commemorate the bravery of the fireman on a Whitemoor to Earls Colne ammunition train that caught fire in the early hours of 2 June 1944 at nearby Soham on the Ely to Newmarket line. Driver Gimbert and Fireman Nightall detached the blazing van and ran it forward to get clear of the town area. Sadly, it exploded in Soham station killing the fireman and signalman and badly injuring the driver; but Soham town was saved from mass destruction by their action. Both men were awarded the George Cross for their bravery. Classmate No 47577 was named *Benjamin Gimbert G.C.* together with 47579 in a dual ceremony at March station on 28 September 1981. The nameplate and plaque were transferred to No 47574 in July 1987.

FORDHAM: The line from Ely through Fordham to Newmarket opened on 1 September 1879. Fordham was the junction for the single line from Cambridge to Mildenhall which opened throughout on 1 April 1885, but was closed to passenger traffic on 18 June 1962 and completely on 13 July 1964. Fordham itself closed as a passenger station on 13 September 1965. This 22 May 1958 view has 'D16/3' 4-4-0 No 62615 leaving on a four-coach Peterborough North to Cambridge via Newmarket train. No 62615 lasted only a little time longer, withdrawal coming on 1 October the same year from March. *G.R. Mortimer*

Twenty-three years later to the day, on 22 May 1991, 'Sprinter' No 156410 passes on the 09.56 Liverpool Lime Street to Ipswich. The main station building is now a private house.

March

MARCH, a small market town with a population of 12,993 in 1960, had an important role as a railway centre. In the 1960s it was approached from five different directions with lines from Spalding, Peterborough, St Ives, Ely and Wisbech. This view of the station was recorded in August 1958 and shows 'B17/6' 4-6-0 No 61642 *Kilverstone Hall* leaving on a train for Ely. This engine had very little time left to run, for withdrawal came on 15 September from Cambridge shed. *P.H. Groom*

There is still a substantial station remaining at March, as this 9 September 1989 view shows. Its importance is now, however, much diminished. Class '47' No 47451 passes through on the 08.20 Liverpool to Norwich.

WHITEMOOR MARSHALLING YARD, March, occupied 68 acres on either side of the ex-Great Northern and Great Eastern joint line to Spalding and Doncaster. The up yard was opened in 1928 and the down in 1931 by the LNER to rationalise freight working around March. Previously four separate yards of pre-Grouping origin and limited capacity were used, which resulted in many uneconomic inter-yard trip workings. Both yards consisted of 10 reception/departure sidings with 42 sorting sidings and were fully mechanised for hump shunting. Alongside the yards was March motive power depot which in May 1960 had an allocation of 103 steam locomotives and 80 diesels. This July 1960 photograph has 'J17' 0-6-0 No 65576 and 'J15' 0-6-0 No 65420 leaving the yard on an afternoon freight to Whittlesea. No 65576, along with 65541 and 65582, was withdrawn on 16 September 1962 from March, the trio being the last survivors of the class. No 65420 was condemned on 1 August the same year, its last shed allocation being Stratford. *John C. Baker*

On 22 May 1991 Class '56' No 56065 arrives on a Redland empties train from Hythe, near Colchester. The former entry and exit lines to Whitemoor Yard are now reduced to just one, the site of the northern end of the yard is now occupied by a prison, and the diesel depot is reduced to a fueling and stabling point only. At the time of writing a large number of withdrawn Class '45' and '47' diesel locomotives are dumped in sidings near the depot.

Wisbech

The line to Wisbech from March opened on 3 May 1847 and was constructed to carry cattle and corn to the harbour. The only intermediate station was Coldham, which closed on 7 March 1966. The line itself closed to passengers on 9 September 1968.

WISBECH on 28 August 1951, and 'D16/3' 4-4-0 No 62531 (withdrawn on 21 March 1955 from Cambridge) leaves the station on the 14.15 Kings Lynn to Cambridge. *LCGB Ken Nunn Collection No 8223*

Wisbech station site is now occupied by private houses and an old people's home, as this 22 May 1991 photograph records. Part of the truncated line still survives south of Wisbech serving a number of industrial locations.

WISBECH & UPWELL TRAMWAY (1): The tramway opened . c on Monday 20 August 1883 as far as Outwell. Built by the Great Eastern Railway, it was a cross between a ventional railway and an urban tramway. Its full $7^3/4$ miles opened to Upwell on Monday 8 September 1884, and passenger services last ran on 31 December 1927, although it continued operation as a freight-only line. After the Second World War it enjoyed a period of great activity from 1945 to 1950 when petrol was rationed, with double- and triple-headed steam-hauled fruit trains of up to 60 vans being common in the season. Steam tram-engines gave way to diesel locomotives in 1952 when the Wisbech allocation ('Y6' No 68083 and 'J70s' 68217/68222/68223/68225) were all placed in store at March shed on 27 July; No 68222 was the last to work the line. The diesel replacements were new Drewry diesel-mechanical 200 hp 0-6-0s, initially Nos 11102 (D2202) and 11103 (D2203). These were joined in August by 11101 (D2201). Traffic declined through the years and the last freight on the line ran on Friday 20 May 1966, worked by D2201, which finished its career as a Crewe Works shunter, being withdrawn on 6 April 1968. This photograph shows 'J70' tram-engine No 68217 running past Brown's New Common Bridge Stores on its way to Upwell in 1951. No 68217 was withdrawn on 9 March 1953 from its store at March. *E.R. Boston Collection*

New Common Bridge Stores has been extensively rebuilt and is now a busy shop and Post Office run by Mr G.W. Brown, the son of the earlier proprietor H.B. Brown. The Wisbech Canal alongside fell into disuse and was drained and filled in. The motor car has triumphed again, for its former course is now a road and is part of the recently improved traffic system around Wisbech. This photograph is dated 22 May 1991.

WISBECH & UPWELL TRAMWAY (2): 'J70' No 68225 is a little further up the line from New Common Bridge on Elm Road, Wisbech, on its way to Upwell, again in 1951. This engine was taken out of store at March and transferred to Ipswich for use in the docks, where it remained until withdrawal on 8 March 1955. *LCGB Ken Nunn Collection No 8219*

New Common Bridge Stores can be seen in the distance on 22 May 1991, but no tram track now survives. The clue that it ran this way is the wide verge alongside a very busy road.

INDEX OF LOCATIONS